# Make your own
# Organic Ice Cream

# Make your own
# Organic Ice Cream
## Using home-grown and local produce

BEN VEAR

SPRING HILL

Published by Spring Hill, an imprint of How To Books Ltd
Spring Hill House, Spring Hill Road
Begbroke, Oxford OX5 1RX
United Kingdom
Tel: (01865) 375794
Fax: (01865) 379162
info@howtobooks.co.uk
www.howtobooks.co.uk

First published 2011

How To Books greatly reduce the carbon footprint of their books by sourcing their typesetting and printing in the UK.

British Library Cataloguing in Publication Data
A catalogue record of this book is available from the British Library.

ISBN: 978 1 905862 75 7

Produced for How To Books by Deer Park Productions, Tavistock, Devon
Designed and typeset by Mousemat Design Ltd
Edited by Jamie Ambrose
Printed and bound by in Great Britain by Bell & Bain Ltd, Glasgow

Ice cream is happiness condensed.
*Jessi Lane Adams*

# Contents

*My great-grandfather Albert Winstone, in his very first ice-cream van, 1952.*

# Introduction

## Hello...

In 1925, my great-grandfather, a gentle, simple and hard-working man named Albert Winstone, used all of his entrepreneurial skills and local connections to start his own ice-cream company, aptly named Winstones Cotswold Ice Cream. When he began, he decided to do something sincere but a bit different: always provide service with a smile and use local goods and services wherever possible to support the community he loved. (No doubt Mary Portas would be proud!)

With the help of his doting wife and close friends, Albert produced all his ice cream on his stove, using an old Victorian recipe he had spent years tweaking and refining. He put freezer blocks in an adapted sidecar and, once the ice cream was loaded into it, set off on his motorcycle around the Cotswolds to sell it, pulling up outside his friends' houses and selling directly to residents, local schools and factories. As the popularity of Albert Winstone's ice cream grew, he began to perfect his vanilla recipe, eventually going on to win a number of national awards.

Nestled among the rolling hills of Gloucestershire, in the heart of the Cotswolds, Winstones Cotswold Ice Cream is still operated by my family from its base on National Trust common land near Stroud. These days our products are distributed around the UK, but we've never lost sight of Great-granddad Bert's original ethos. The company he founded continues to use only the finest Cotswold water, local organic milk and double cream from a beautiful herd of shorthorn cows, which graze on grassland just a mile from the Winstones' factory and parlour. My mother, father, brother and I now run things, and we're still champions of local food. Whenever possible we forage for the fruits and herbs we use in our kitchen, as well as shopping at the fantastic Stroud Farmers' Market and in a number of the delis and farm stores dotted around the county.

For many years the recipes used and developed by my great-grandfather Albert and his son (my grandfather Frank) remained locked in an old iron safe that sat rather unloved at the bottom of a beautiful cottage garden in Rodborough, next to the family

*My great-grandfather Albert Winstone, founder of Winstones Cotswold Ice Cream, serving ice cream to local children, 1932.*

*Albert's brother-in-law Lewis Cook, serving ice cream to his daughter and my great-aunt Mavis, late 1930s.*

firm and ice cream factory-cum-parlour. Not having seen the light of day for years, these recipes gathered dust in the slowly aging safe, which languished stoically through wind, rain, snow and sunshine for half a century – until a few years ago, when I stumbled across it while foraging the wild hedgerow at the bottom of my grandfather's garden one balmy summer evening.

Amazed by the size and stature of the safe, my curiosity got the better of me. Thanks to the amount of rust that had accumulated, the hinges had warped and were very weak, so I managed to force open the door. Not knowing what to expect, I ran my hand across two shelves inside and brushed off a thick coating of dust to reveal a pile of papers and photographs (some of which can be seen throughout this book) bundled together with a length of string. After studying these over a few cups of fresh coffee, I was overjoyed to discover the original ice-cream recipes developed by Great-grandfather Albert in the 1920s, when he first set up Winstones Cotswold Ice Cream. Gradually, I realised that these images and recipes hadn't been seen for over half a century – a time of huge change locally, nationally and globally.

It struck me that these recipes, which have been enjoyed by countless people through the years, should be shared and enjoyed by all. Thus I felt inspired, and my own adventure to write a cookery book began! The recipes were just the starting point, though; after more than 85 years of business, I also thought it was about time to share all we've learned about the food we love and the ice cream we make, so I wrote it down – here, in this book. When recreating the recipes, I found that, while many of them were delicious, some required a small number of changes to bring them up to date, while others have provided the base for newly developed recipes, such as Guinness Ice Cream (see page 90) and Gin & Tonic Sorbet (see page 142).

At first, people asked me why I would want to share such recipes with the outside world. Countless friends warned me against it, remarking that 'If another ice-cream company gets hold of those, then...' But ice-cream recipes are easy to come by. The difference with our family's recipes is the high quality of ingredients they use, the simple and straightforward method of production, and the delicious flavours. To me, these are all reasons why the recipes should be shared.

Where feasible when making any of the ice-cream recipes in this book, I encourage you to buy ingredients from local producers, and preferably organic. Those that contribute to your own local community and operate on a fair and ethical basis are worth supporting as much as possible. Enjoy!

## My ethos

I've grown up around food, and it's pretty much my life. However, I don't want to preach. No doubt you're aware of the importance of supporting your local producers, independent shops and artisans. From endless articles in the news to television shows like *Jamie's Food Revolution* and *The People's Supermarket*, I'm sure you've already been converted to the growing local food movement. So without prattling on for pages and pages, I hope that when sourcing your ingredients you will remember the importance of seasonality and provenance as well as the small farms, delis, greengrocers and market-stallholders that rely on your custom.

Whenever possible I shop locally. This means buying from my fantastic local farmers' market, delis and local producers, and through farm shops and delicatessens in and around the Cotswolds. It's a practice that helps support my local community, local jobs and the high street.

In the countryside, this is fairly easy; many people would even suggest that we countryside-dwelling folks have a slower pace of life than those in, say, central London. I agree, and it can sometimes prove a little trickier in the city to get really fresh, local produce. But if you explore, I'm sure you'll come across some great markets and delis in your own neighbourhood.

I'm not suggesting that you shouldn't shop in your local supermarket, by the way. That isn't realistic. After all, supermarkets are often low-cost and very convenient, but whenever possible, I do encourage you simply to try and support local sources for greater variety, seasonal food, great taste and as an aid to your local economy.

As well as keeping it local, keep it simple. If a recipe is too difficult or creates too much mess, then by all means, feel free to simplify it to suit your needs. Food is meant to be *enjoyed* – not laboured over. As such, the recipes in this book avoid the complex (and often dull) language found in cookery books, especially where desserts and ice cream are concerned.

Remember that cooking should never be a chore, or strenuous. It should be fun, relaxing, enjoyable – even a social occasion. So at dinner parties especially, be sure to get your family, friends or even neighbours round to pitch in, especially when it's time to do the washing up!

# How It All Began

Growing up in the small but perfectly formed Cotswold town of Nailsworth, I had a childhood completely surrounded by food. Easter and summer holidays were spent with my sweet little gran, at her rickety house just down a short, dusty track from my grandfather's ice-cream business.

During those long, balmy summers I played with my brother and cousins on the National Trust common land that borders my grandparents' home. There was always something to do: explore the local wildlife, play hide-and-seek in the leafy woodland, endlessly run in and out of my grandfather's shop. It was great – especially having ice cream virtually on tap, although at the time I had very little appreciation for what I was scoffing and plastering on my T-shirts and face (much to my mother's despair). On a final-year secondary-school trip to Italy, however, I spent several weeks travelling the great cities of Florence, Venice and Rome, and my eyes were truly opened to the world of sweet treats, great food and ice cream. For the first time, I began to take note of what I was eating, where it had come from and what went into it. During this and successive trips to Italy, I discovered that ice cream is truly steeped in history.

## A brief history of ice cream

While it has been the lifeblood of my family for generations, ice cream's history is many thousands of years older. Most historians agree that ancient civilisations in Rome, Greece, Persia and the powerful dynasties of China probably served chilled and ice-cold sweetened foods, storing the ice needed to make them in great stone ice houses during the hot summer months. These were the forerunners of modern-day ice cream and ice-based desserts.

According to some records, for example, the Roman emperor Nero had slaves bring ice from the mountains, which was then kept in ice houses and eventually combined with fruit toppings, honey and even sweet nectar to make some of the earliest chilled delicacies. Much later the Arabs began to use milk as a chief ingredient in the production of sweet ice- and cream-based desserts; they sweetened chilled cream with sugar rather than fruit juices.

True ice cream, as it's served today, is thought to have been created during the eighteenth century in both England and America. One of the first recipes for it appeared in London in 1733, in a book called *Mrs. Mary Eales's Receipts*. This particular recipe is still a favourite of top chefs like Heston Blumenthal, and it reads as follows:

> *To ice cream. Take Tin Ice-Pots, fill them with any Sort of Cream you like, either plain or sweeten'd, or Fruit in it; shut your Pots very close; to six Pots you must allow eighteen or twenty Pound of Ice, breaking the Ice very small; there will be some great Pieces, which lay at the Bottom and Top: You must have a Pail, and lay some Straw at the Bottom; then lay in your Ice, and put in amongst it a Pound of Bay-Salt; set in your Pots of Cream, and lay Ice and Salt between every Pot, that they may not touch; but the Ice must lie round them on every Side; lay a good deal of Ice on the Top, cover the Pail with Straw, set it in a Cellar where no Sun or Light comes, it will be froze in four Hours, but it may stand longer; than take it out just as you use it; hold it in your Hand and it will slip out.*

By the middle of the nineteenth century, several different amateur chefs had developed a number of different ice-cream recipes varying in flavour, style and consistency. By this time, too, better techniques of commercial ice-cream manufacturing had also been invented, which reduced the cost of ice cream to the public and increased its presence in towns and cities.

In the UK, however, ice cream remained expensive right up until the late 1800s, but this began to change when large quantities of ice were brought into the country from northern Europe and the United States.

During the twentieth century, ice cream really came into its own in terms of availability through networks of vendors, ice-cream parlours and street traders. The emergence of a wide range of new flavours helped the product grow in popularity as a desirable treat, both on its own and in new and exciting dishes. For instance, the ice-cream soda became a favourite at 'soda fountains' and ice-cream parlours in the US. During the Prohibition era, the 'Coke Float', made of Coca-Cola and a scoop (or two) of vanilla ice cream, gained a huge following.

Once refrigeration became affordable in the mid-twentieth century, frozen desserts such as ice cream exploded in popularity, and sparked a huge growth in the number of ice-cream stores as well as flavours and types. Sellers often competed with each other on the basis of the varieties they sold.

Yet perhaps the most important development in ice-cream production arrived in UK during the 1950s, with the introduction of soft ice-cream machines. At its heart, soft ice cream consists essentially a base mixture of cream (or in some modern cases, fat), sugar, milk and flavouring, all pumped up with air to give it a soft, light consistency. When a team of British research chemists (which included a young Margaret Thatcher) discovered a way to double the amount of air, this meant that manufacturers could use fewer ingredients.

While it sounds like a money-making scam, the project was originally commissioned by the British government in order to tackle the milk shortage that had resulted from rationing in World War II. In its early years, soft-serve 'whippy' ice cream was seen simply as a way of making milk go further – and getting more calcium into British children's diets.

The 1980s – the decade of big hair, the New Romantic movement and some absolute fashion faux pas – witnessed a return to thicker, cream-based ice cream sold at a premium in a whole host of spectacular and very Eighties' flavours, such as 'Tutti-frutti', 'Peaches & Cream' and 'Turkish Delight' – all of which are considered fairly outdated by today's standards. By the end of the 1980s, too, the demise of ice-cream vans out on rounds was fast approaching. In many senses this was a sign of the times, much like the death of the milkman and his milk round, hastened along by the rapid growth of big supermarkets in the UK.

This situation isn't likely to go away any time soon, but to be fair, it isn't all doom and gloom. What's exciting for an artisan ice-cream maker and cook like myself is the general public's growing awareness of the provenance of food. These days consumers are eager to know more about the production process, and where their food comes from. Unsung food heroes in pockets around the country such as Rob Rees, Tom Herbert and Emily Knight have increased awareness of food issues within our local communities, encouraging shoppers to support their independent producers and retailers. Also, celebrity chefs such as Gordon Ramsay, Hugh Fearnley-Whittingstall, Rick Stein and Willie Harcourt-Cooze have focused mass attention on issues surrounding food, really kick-starting a growing food revolution and the revival of Great British Food – in particular dessert and dairy-based goods.

As part of this 'new movement' myself, over the next few pages I'll be sharing with you some of my family's favourite and most famous recipes, which have sat locked in my grandfather's safe for more than half a century. Because you will be making ice cream in a kitchen rather than in a factory environment, the method used to produce Winstones Cotswold Ice Cream is, of course, drastically different to what you'll read here; however, the ingredients, principle and ethos remain the same.

And trust me: you'll be really pleased with the results!

# The science behind ice cream

At school, science and maths were never my strong suit, as I'm sure my teachers and parents would tell you! However, much like Heston Blumenthal or Bompas & Parr, when it comes to food, science takes on a whole new meaning for me. Creating new flavours, adjusting the properties of taste and texture and developing new recipes have become keen interests of mine, with ice cream, of course, being a particular fascination.

The secret of making fantastic ice cream, both commercially and at home, is having a correct balance of ingredients – sugar, fat, total solids and liquid – to ensure that the ice cream freezes and is scoop-able. Otherwise your recipe is likely to create a dessert with a grainy texture.

In essence, milk-based ice cream contains a mixture of air, fat globules, ice crystals and liquids. The way in which the water within these liquid ingredients (milk, fruit, cream, alcohol) freezes, combines and interacts with other ingredients is what ensures that all ice creams take on different characters.

Adding sugar to ice cream ensures that it is sweet and has good stability and body (making it scoop-able). It also helps to dissolve some of the liquid ingredients used, which balances the recipe, and influences the freezing point of ice cream, lowering the freezing temperature. In the case of sorbets and alcoholic-based ice creams, sugar makes sure the mixture will actually freeze in both a standard home freezer or huge commercial cold store.

Arguably, egg is perhaps the most important ingredient in any ice-cream mixture. It not only acts as a stabiliser, but it also emulsifies the mixture by joining fat globules with liquid water, preventing the classic 'oil and water' separation.

While sugar helps to sweeten and stabilise the ice-cream mix, adding air means that the mixture isn't too dense, giving it a light, creamy texture. The addition of air also separates fat globules and ice crystals, ensuring that the ice cream has the correct texture and isn't just a block of ice.

To sum up, a balance of solids and liquids with the addition of air gives ice cream the perfect texture. This should be solid, but at the same time scoop-able and stable. In the event that any ice cream you make isn't stable – for example, if it melts very quickly, is difficult to scoop or has an unpleasant texture – consider adding a small amount of alcohol if it's too hard, or water if the mixture is too soft.

# The Basics

## Equipment

**Do I need an ice-cream maker?**

Whenever I run courses or give someone a smoothie or ice-cream recipe, people usually assume they might have to buy some wildly expensive kitchen gizmos to achieve the desired result. This isn't the case at all. While you will need some relatively inexpensive equipment (pots and pans, utensils, etc.) which you most likely already own, an ice-cream maker isn't essential; it just makes things quicker and a little more consistent – after all, simple cooking is what I'm all about. At home I use a Magimix Gelato, which retails at under £250; however, there are a number of other home ice-cream makers that retail at around £50.

If you simply can't afford an ice-cream maker, don't have the space in your kitchen or aren't sure if you'll use it enough to warrant the expense, then almost all the ice cream and sorbet recipes in this book can be put into the freezer and hand-churned every hour (and each recipe spells out exactly how to do this). This process should be repeated at least three times before the mixture is left another hour to set and – *voilà!* – is ready to serve.

For a number of ice cream and sorbet flavours and smoothies, I do, however, suggest that you purchase a blender. If your budget allows, then a juicer is also a great help. These machines don't have to be flash; one of your friends or family members might even have a blender or juicer gathering dust in a cupboard somewhere, so they might lend it to you. It never hurts to ask!

> ## CHEF'S TIP
> ### Making ice cream by hand
> *Pour your cooled ice-cream mixture into a freezer-proof container, cover it securely with a lid and put it in the freezer. Remove it from the freezer after 1 hour to whisk, then replace. This prevents large ice crystals from forming and should be repeated 3 times before leaving the ice cream in the freezer to set.*

## The kit

### *Our juicer*

Over the years, being a fairly health-conscious family, we have used a lot (and I mean a LOT) of different juicers. In fact, that's all I wanted for my twelfth birthday – a little odd for a 12-year-old, I know, but I did lose interest fairly quickly and returned to my stack of *Star Wars* videos.

You could pop to your local high street or virtually any department or kitchen or homewares store and spend a vast sum of money on a shiny new juicer, but ours, a second-hand Philips HR1861, cost us just over £25, and it does the job. It squeezes all

of the juice out of oranges, pears, apples and any other type of vegetable or fruit. Sure, it isn't all stainless steel and shiny, and it's certainly no bold fashion statement, but I rather like its shabby white plastic exterior. Otherwise, Russell Hobbs and Andrew James make similar and very popular models.

## Our ice-cream maker

Well, we have a factory's worth of machinery, and if you're ever in the neighbourhood, please do drop in for a visit. Everything in there is neatly ordered, spotlessly clean and made from stainless steel.

My own kitchen, of course, is another matter. There are no vast stainless-steel machines and it's not always spotlessly clean. My home ice-cream maker is a Magimix Gelato that cost me about £200 from Amazon. But other makers are available for around £60, which seems like a fairly affordable price. Whatever type you purchase, ensure that your ice-cream maker is dishwasher-friendly (that's very important!). But remember: this isn't an essential piece of kit; it just makes life a bit easier (which is what we like). As mentioned already, almost all of my ice-cream recipes can be churned by hand to break up ice crystals, then placed in the freezer.

## Our blender

This kitchen gizmo is my all-time favourite. It's a complete rock in my kitchen, upon which, as you will see, almost all of my recipes rely.

I currently use a Philips 750W Aluminium Blender. It looks very pretty (it has flashing blue lights!) and set me back about £60 in the John Lewis January sale. Not wanting to sound like a television advert, it's available from all good retailers. I love this blender in particular because:

- it has a 2.5-litre glass jug – very solid and very dishwasher-friendly;
- it has a sturdy base made from brushed aluminium (looks very sleek);
- it has three main settings: Smoothie, Pulse and Ice; and
- it's wildly powerful at 750 watts. Don't settle for less than 500 or you will struggle to crush fruit and ice.

## Other stuff

It goes without saying that you need a hob on which to heat your ice-cream custards and sorbet bases. Along with the gizmos already mentioned you'll also need:

- a couple of sharp knives,
- a good solid chopping board,
- an ice-cream scoop,
- some plastic freezer-safe containers,
- a mixing bowl,
- a whisk, and
- a set of pots and pans.

Oh, and remember to check that all your equipment likes going in the dishwasher – to cut down on mess-induced stress.

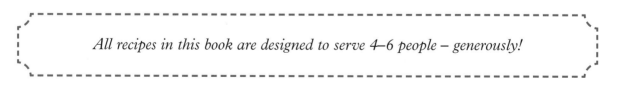

*All recipes in this book are designed to serve 4–6 people – generously!*

# Ingredients

Below is a fairly exhaustive list of the ingredients I've used throughout the book, so use it as a rough guide when buying your own ingredients. You may wish to add additions after tasting and testing, or to explore new flavours. For each category, though, please try, whenever possible, to support your local markets and producers. And if the budget allows, choose organic ingredients.

## Alcohol

Peter at the Bristol Cider Shop has been my chief advisor when it comes to ciders, perries and wine; really, you should choose the brands that most appeal to you and fit your budget. Where spirits have been used (vodka, Cointreau and gin), I've attempted to source the best-possible artisan brands, such as William Chase's groundbreaking potato-based Chase Vodka.

## Chocolate

Buying good-quality organic or Fairtrade chocolate is not as straightforward as you might think. It's very important that you purchase a chocolate that is no less than 60 per cent cocoa solids. Green & Blacks and Willie's Cacao are particularly good, but I've found Divine 70 per cent and 85 per cent chocolate to be the best and have used these throughout in all of my recipes.

## Dairy products

Essential ingredients for ice cream are, of course, milk and cream. When making ice cream both at home and at Winstones Cotswold Ice Cream I source my dairy goods from Woefuldane Organics, a local organic farm based near the town of Minchinhampton, Gloucestershire. Its dairy products are produced by the farm's small herd of 50 home-bred traditional dairy shorthorn cows. Shorthorn cows were the backbone of dairy farming in rural England for hundreds of years, and the shorthorn breed is perfect for a truly organic farming regime.

## Eggs

My eggs come from old Cotswold legbar hens based just miles from my home, based on a beautiful farm overlooking the historic town of Broadway. These Gloucestershire hens live a rather peaceful life, wandering freely around natural grassland without a care in the world. Their beautiful eggs have a soft, blue-coloured shell and complement any meal fantastically. All of my recipes use large, organic eggs.

## Fruit and foraging

Where possible, between the months of June and November I forage in hedgerows and common land for gooseberries, redcurrants, blackberries, raspberries, apples, cherry plums, elderflower, mint and even some more interesting and rare (but equally as delicious) wild fruits such as loganberries and whitecurrants. Your hedgerows may not offer you exactly the same fruits, but have a go and see what you can find! Whenever I haven't been able to source my own fruits and herbs, I turn to my local fruit farms in Cheltenham or visit regular weekend farmers' markets held throughout Cotswold towns. You can do the same in your own local area.

## Herbs and spices

In my recipes I've used basil, thyme, sage, mint, nutmeg, saffron and cloves. I try to grow all of my herbs in my herb garden and window boxes, but if you have neither the time nor space to do this, then you can find most of these in the herb and spice section of any good deli or supermarket.

## Vegetables

In my savoury recipes I have used a range of vegetables which may, in some cases, prove slightly difficult to sources locally. When this happens, I turn to my local supermarket. However, all of my tomatoes are grown by my mother and grandfather in their vegetable patches.

## Honey

All of the honey used throughout this book is natural, thick and local, bought from the Cheltenham-based Gusto Italian Delicatessen and Italian Caffe. Local honey is readily available from your own local deli or market stall. Look for orange blossom or any other clear, thick honey.

## Water

We often take water very much for granted, but when creating high-quality sorbets I use Cotswold spring water, a naturally filtered spring water. If you want to source your own spring water to use, then beware of some bottled waters that may have been shipped from overseas. It just doesn't make sense to me!

## Additional ingredients

Additional ingredients that I haven't produced, foraged or made myself are always purchased responsibly from local delis, farmers' markets or directly from producers.

# Making the Perfect Custard

A number of the seasonal flavours found in this book are made using the same (or very similar) basic techniques and methods. In some cases like Strawberry (see page 36) and Blackberries & Cream (page 42), this has been done with additions such as different fruit and ingredients. To avoid repetition, then, the basic ice-cream custard and method used in all these recipes is shown in the following pages.

When making ice cream, you essentially create a custard, then add different levels of sugar, fruit, herbs, alcohol and flavourings in different measures, according to the type of ice cream you want to make. Whatever type you're making, though, it's essential not to burn the custard or heat it too quickly; otherwise, you're likely to end up with a scrambled-egg-type mixture that will have both an unpleasant taste and texture.

Cream must also be heated slowly, with continuous stirring, in order to avoid burning and separating the mixture. In the event that you do burn or heat your custard too quickly, however, don't panic! Rescue advice is given on page 27.

Remember where possible to support your local markets and producers as far as ingredients are concerned, and if your budget allows, always choose organic alternatives.

*All recipes in this chapter are designed to serve 4–6 people – generously!*

# Basic Custard

When working with food – particularly with eggs and dairy goods – hygiene is vitally important. So as a first step in the process, I advise sterilising all of your equipment in hot, soapy water.
This custard will keep in the freezer for 3 months but don't take it out and then refreeze it.

250ml organic double cream
300ml organic full-fat milk
120g Fairtrade caster sugar
3 large organic egg yolks

1. Pour the cream and milk into a medium or large heavy-based pan (ensure that it's dishwasher-friendly) over a low heat.

❋

2. Tip in half the sugar, stirring at regular intervals.
Don't allow the mixture to boil.

❋

3. Whisk the egg yolks and the remaining sugar in a heatproof mixing bowl, beating with an electric whisk for about 2 minutes, or until the mixture has thickened like custard.

❋

4. Pour the hot milk and cream into the eggs, then return the mixture to the pan and put it back on a low heat, stir constantly to avoid burning.

❋

5. Heat gently, still stirring, for approximately 10 minutes, until the mixture has a thick, custard-like consistency. Make sure it doesn't boil – as soon as you see any bubbles about to burst to the surface, it should be thick enough.

❋

6. Remove from the heat so that the mixture doesn't curdle and set aside for 10 minutes before putting the custard in the fridge to chill.

❋

7. Turn on your ice cream machine and, once up and running, slowly pour in the chilled mixture. Follow your manufacturer's instructions and leave it to churn.

✳

8. When it stops, the ice cream will probably be too soft to eat, so spoon it into a plastic or freezer-safe container, seal the lid firmly and freeze for a minimum of 2 hours, or overnight. Remove from the freezer 15 minutes before serving to soften slightly (so as to not break your wrist or scoop) and bingo!

### To make basic custard by hand

1. Heat the milk and half the sugar without the cream (the custard will be slightly thicker). Follow the rest of the method steps until step 6.

✳

2. At the start of step 6, whip the cream until it's light and floppy but not too stiff, then fold it into the cold custard.

✳

3. Put into a freezer-proof container and seal the lid firmly. Place in the freezer for 3-4 hours, stirring once an hour to aerate the ice cream and prevent the formation of large ice crystals.

✳

4. Repeat this 3 times, then leave the ice cream to freeze solid. This method is hassle-free and will ensure your ice cream is smooth and dreamy.

## CHEF'S TIP
### Rescuing custard when things go wrong
*If you allow the custard to boil, or if it curdles – which may happen, for example, if you add too much lemon juice too quickly – then it can be rescued. Pour the mixture into a blender or use a hand blender or electric whisk and vigorously whisk the custard until it binds together again.*

*My great-grandmother Doris, with Albert's brother-in-law Terry Gillman, taking a break from ice-cream making in early 1950.*

# Basic Flavours

As a family business in the heart of the serene Cotswolds we enjoy our simpler, slower way of life. In keeping with this simplicity, I ensure that my cookery isn't overly pretentious or difficult, and that it can be put into practice by anyone, from an amateur to a professional cook, at home or commercially.

The recipes in this chapter build upon the basic technique and recipe shown on pages 26–7. Here you'll find a number of simple, easy-to-make basic recipes ranging from Bourbon Vanilla, Chocolate and Dairy through to Mint Choc Chip and Strawberry. Once you've mastered making these basic flavours, you can, if you wish, begin to experiment with different fruits, spices and herbs as well as textures and the addition of other ingredients such as chocolate chips, toffee pieces and fruit.

Most of the recipes in this chapter and throughout the book are custard-based ice creams, which I prefer. This custard base has been used in my family for almost a century, but it's also known more commonly as French-custard-style ice cream. French-custard-style ice cream is typically rich and smooth, and it lends itself well to flavours such as chocolate, vanilla, clove and Guinness, but less so to fruit-based types such as strawberry, lemon and blackberry.

In addition to the French-style ice creams in the book, I've included a number of fruit-based recipes that follow a technique known as the Philadelphia style of ice-cream making, typically used in my fruit-based recipes. Philadelphia-style ice cream uses a combination of milk, cream and sugar; unlike French-style ice cream, it doesn't contain eggs.

*All recipes in this chapter are designed to serve 4–6 people – generously!*

# Traditional Vanilla Ice Cream

Great-grandfather Albert started out by making vanilla ice cream from a Victorian recipe. This is my family's staple, bread-and-butter flavour, and has been for close to a century. It's smooth, and its creamy texture is enhanced with a subtle vanilla flavour. Do enjoy!

350ml organic double cream
300ml organic full-fat milk
120g Fairtrade caster sugar
1 vanilla pod, sliced lengthways
5 large organic egg yolks

1. Pour the cream and milk into a medium or large heavy-based dishwasher-friendly pan. Tip in half the sugar and the vanilla pod and cook gently over a low heat, stirring at regular intervals and not allowing the mixture to boil.

✳

2. Whisk the egg yolks and the remaining sugar in a heatproof mixing bowl, beating with an electric whisk for about 2 minutes, or until the mixture has thickened like custard.

✳

3. Combine both mixtures and return the pan to a low heat. Cook, stirring all the time, for approximately 10 minutes, until the mixture takes on a thick, custard-like consistency. Make sure it doesn't boil; as soon as you see any bubbles about to burst to the surface, it should be thick enough, so take the pan off the heat immediately to ensure the mixture doesn't curdle. Set aside to cool.

✳

4. Remove the vanilla pod from the mixture, then pour it into your ice-cream maker, follow the manufacturer's instructions and leave to churn. (Alternatively, pour the mixture into a freezer-proof container, seal it firmly with a lid and place in the freezer. Whisk after 1 hour to prevent ice crystals from forming; repeat 3 times before leaving it to set.)

✳

5. When the churning stops, the ice cream will probably be too soft to eat, so spoon it into a plastic or freezer-safe container and freeze.

✳

6. Remove from the freezer 15 minutes before serving to soften slightly (that way you won't break your wrist or scoop).
Bingo! Home-made vanilla ice cream!

# Bourbon Vanilla Ice Cream

A slightly richer, and more luxury version of my great-grandfather's recipe, Bourbon Vanilla is smooth, sweet and totally delicious. Adjust the vanilla flavour according to your own personal taste.

350ml organic double cream
300ml organic full-fat milk
120g Fairtrade caster sugar
1 vanilla pod
3 large organic egg yolks
1 tbsp Madagascar bourbon vanilla extract

1. Pour the cream and milk into a medium or large heavy-based dishwasher-friendly pan, tip in half the sugar and vanilla pod and cook over a low heat, stirring at regular intervals. Do not allow the mixture to boil.

✳

2. Whisk the egg yolks and the remaining sugar in a mixing bowl, beating with an electric whisk for about 2 minutes, or until the mixture has thickened like custard.

✳

3. Combine both mixtures and the vanilla extract, return the pan to a low heat and cook, stirring all the time, for approximately 10 minutes, until the mixture takes on a thick, custard-like consistency. Make sure it doesn't boil; as soon as you see any bubbles about to burst to the surface, it should be thick enough, so take the pan off the heat to prevent curdling. Set aside to cool.

✳

4. Scoop out the vanilla pod from the mixture, pour it into your ice-cream maker, follow the manufacturer's instructions and leave to churn. (Alternatively, pour the mixture into a freezer-proof container, seal it firmly with a lid and place in the freezer. Whisk after 1 hour to prevent ice crystals from forming; repeat 3 times before leaving it to set.)

✳

5. When the ice-cream maker stops, the ice cream is probably too soft to eat, so spoon it into a plastic or freezer-safe container. Remember to remove it from the freezer 15 minutes before serving to soften slightly, so as to not break your wrist or scoop!

# Dairy Ice Cream

Dairy ice cream is perhaps one of the most popular flavours on the market, reminiscent of summer holidays by the seaside or abroad, often in the blazing heat. It's what people think of when they think of a dipping cone or '99'. This is another very old family recipe, used by Great-granddad Albert. It uses the same method as the Traditional Vanilla recipe on page 30, but replaces the vanilla pod with a spoonful of clotted cream.

300ml organic double cream
400ml organic full-fat milk
120g Fairtrade golden caster sugar
2 large spoonfuls of really thick clotted cream
4 large organic egg yolks

1. Pour the cream and milk into a medium or large heavy-based dishwasher-friendly pan. Tip in half the sugar and clotted cream and cook over a low heat, stirring at regular intervals. Do not allow the mixture to boil.

❄

2. Whisk the egg yolks and the remaining sugar in a heatproof mixing bowl, beating with an electric whisk for about 2 minutes, or until the mixture has thickened like custard.

❄

3. Combine both mixtures, return the pan to a low heat and cook, stirring all the time, for approximately 10 minutes, or until the mixture takes on a thick, custard-like consistency. Make sure it doesn't boil. As soon as you see any bubbles about to burst to the surface, it should be thick enough, so take the pan off the heat to prevent curdling. Set aside to cool.

❄

4. Pour the mixture into your ice-cream maker, follow the manufacturer's instructions and leave to churn. (Alternatively, pour the mixture into a freezer-proof container, seal it firmly with a lid and place in the freezer. Whisk after 1 hour to prevent ice crystals from forming; repeat 3 times before leaving it to set.) While waiting, sit back and enjoy life!

❄

5. When the churning has finished, put the ice cream in a freezer-proof container and freeze it for 1 hour to ensure that it's firm. Remove from the freezer 15 minutes before serving to allow the ice cream to soften.

# Chocolate Ice Cream

Chocolate is the ultimate luxury food, originating from the ancient civilisations of South America. Some fantastic artisan chocolate producers and products are available these days, not only in your local deli and farm shop but also in supermarkets up and down the UK. This is thanks largely to chefs and businesspeople such as Willie Harcourt-Cooze of Willie's Cacao and Craig Sams of Green & Black's, who have championed the use of high-quality, organic chocolate in cooking. Here I favour the use of Divine Chocolate, which produces delicious, Fairtrade chocolate as part of a cooperative where the farmers own 40 per cent of the business – genius!

200ml organic double cream
200ml organic full-fat milk
150g Fairtrade caster sugar
100g chocolate (at least 70%), roughly chopped
1 large organic egg yolk

1. Pour the cream and milk into a dishwasher-friendly saucepan, then tip in half the sugar and all the chocolate. Put the pan over a low heat, stirring at regular intervals, and allowing the chocolate to melt but not boil or burn.

❋

2. Whisk the egg yolk and the remaining sugar in a heatproof mixing bowl, beating with an electric whisk for about 2 minutes, or until the mixture thickens to a smooth paste.

❋

3. Combine both mixtures and return the pan to a low heat. Cook, stirring constantly, for approximately 10 minutes, or until thick and custard-like in consistency. When the custard coats the back of your spoon, it's ready!

❋

4. Set the mixture aside to chill in the refrigerator. After half an hour, pour the mixture into your ice-cream maker, follow the manufacturer's instructions and leave to churn. (Alternatively, pour the mixture into a freezer-proof container, seal it firmly with a lid and place in the freezer. Whisk after 1 hour to prevent ice crystals from forming; repeat 3 times before leaving it to set.) While waiting, sit back and enjoy life!

❋

5. When the churning has finished, put the ice cream in a freezer-proof container and freeze it for 1 hour to ensure that it's firm.

# Strawberry Ice Cream

Strawberries are the ultimate summer fruit: intense in colour, texture and taste, a perfect balance of sweet and tart. For this recipe I've used cream from a local organic farm, Woefuldane, which is based on ancient grassland in the heart of the Cotswolds. Their herd of 100 shorthorn cows are lovingly cared for in beautiful surroundings. My strawberries, picked from the local pick-your-own at Primrose Vale fruit farm, near Cheltenham, help to create this great summer-flavoured ice cream – perfect for the Wimbledon season!

1 large organic egg
150g Fairtrade caster sugar
300g strawberries
Dash of lemon juice
150ml organic full-fat milk
100ml organic double cream

1. In a heatproof mixing bowl, beat the egg and sugar together using a hand whisk until they form a pale, smooth paste.

❋

2. In a blender, whizz up the strawberries with a dash of lemon juice until the mixture is completely liquid. Set aside to allow the flavours to infuse.

❋

3. Pour the milk and cream into a saucepan, put it over a low heat and bring it to a simmer, stirring constantly to avoid burning.

❋

4. Pour the hot milk and cream over the egg mixture, then stir in the strawberry purée. Scrape the bottom of the pan to ensure the mixture has combined before setting it aside to chill in the fridge.

❋

5. Once the mixture has chilled for at least half an hour, pour it into your ice-cream maker. Follow the manufacturer's instructions and leave to churn. (Alternatively, pour the mixture into a freezer-proof container, seal it firmly with a lid and place in the freezer. Whisk after 1 hour to prevent ice crystals from forming; repeat 3 times before leaving it to set.) When it has finished churning, it will probably be too soft to eat, so spoon it into a freezer-safe container and put in the freezer to firm up.

❋

6. Remove from the freezer 15 minutes before serving to soften slightly.

# Mint Choc Chip Ice Cream

There must be something about the colour green; when friends and family bring their kids to our ice-cream parlour, Mint Choc Chip is, hands down, the most popular flavour of the day.

250ml organic full-fat milk
150g Fairtrade caster sugar
400ml organic double cream
80g fresh mint leaves (roughly 2 handfuls)
5 large organic egg yolks
50g chocolate chips

1. In a saucepan, gently heat the milk, half of the sugar and all the cream. Bring it up to a simmer before adding roughly 2 handfuls of mint leaves. Set on a low heat, stir the mixture and allow the flavours to infuse for up to 1 hour.

✳

2. Set aside to cool, then strain the mixture through a fine strainer and discard the mint leaves.

✳

3. In a separate saucepan, whisk the yolks and remaining sugar together until they take on a smooth, pale consistency. Put the egg mixture over a low heat, slowly pour in the mint mixture and stir vigorously.

✳

4. Continue to heat the ice-cream mixture until it begins to thicken; once it's thick enough to coat the back of your spoon, it's ready. Set aside to cool.

✳

5. Stir in a few handfuls of chocolate chips and chill in the fridge before pouring the mixture into your ice-cream maker. Follow the manufacturer's instructions and leave to churn. (Alternatively, pour the mixture into a freezer-proof container, seal it firmly with a lid and place in the freezer. Whisk after 1 hour to prevent ice crystals from forming; repeat 3 times before leaving it to set.)

## CHEF'S TIP
### Achieving the perfect colour
*If you prefer a vivid green colour in your Mint Choc Chip Ice Cream, add a few teaspoons of crème de menthe.*

# Spring & Summer Flavours

In the words of Jessi Lane Adams, 'Ice cream is happiness condensed.' That being the case, when better to enjoy a scoop of ice cream bursting with flavour than during the spring and summer months? Sunshine is really what ice cream is all about. I'm never sure whether it's the weather, the UV rays shining down on us, good company or even just good food, but the summer really is a time to enjoy with friends and family.

To reflect this theme, this chapter includes a number of flavours that are reminiscent of summer, featuring seasonal fruit and herbs that can be easily foraged in your local area or found at your local farm shop, delicatessen or market stall. Flavours such as Blackberries & Cream, Raspberry, British Summer Hedgerow and Pimm's all make for a delicious treat on a long, hot summer's day – and a glass of wine is recommended, too!

The recipes in this chapter have been made using both the French-custard and the Philadelphia style of ice-cream production, which lend themselves well to fruit- and confectionery-based recipes and flavours.

*All recipes in this chapter are designed to serve 4–6 people – generously!*

CHEF'S TIP
Foraging for fruits
*Be respectful of the countryside when you're out and about foraging for fruits from hedgerows. Take only what you need and try to leave the hedgerows and wild fruit trees as you find them.*

# Blackberries & Cream Ice Cream

From late August to early September, hedgerows around the countryside are literally buckling under the weight of fresh, ripe blackberries, ready for picking and perfect for cooking. Keen fans of blackberries, my grandparents used to take my brother and me on what seemed like endless rambles around the common land adjoining their house, stopping every few hundred metres to pick blackberries and raspberries from the brambles. This recipe brings back the memories of those sweet, fruit-laden days.

300g blackberries
3 tbsp fresh lemon juice
150g Fairtrade caster sugar
200ml organic full-fat milk
100ml organic double cream

1. In a blender, whizz together the blackberries, lemon juice, sugar and milk, until the mixture is a smooth liquid.

❋

2. In a medium saucepan, heat the cream over a gentle heat. Add the sugar and the blackberry mixture and cook for approximately 10 minutes, being careful not to boil the mixture to avoid 'cream-curdling'.

❋

3. Allow the mixture to cool before pouring it into your ice-cream maker. Follow the manufacturer's instructions and leave to churn. (Alternatively, pour the mixture into a freezer-proof container, seal it firmly with a lid and place in the freezer. Whisk after 1 hour to prevent ice crystals from forming; repeat 3 times before leaving it to set).

❋

4. Place in the freezer to let the ice cream firm up before serving.

## CHEF'S TIP
### Leftover fruit
*Don't throw away any leftover blackberries you might have in the fridge – especially after all that foraging!* *Turn to page 179 to find out how to make a delicious Blackberry, Raspberry & Blueberry Smoothie.*

# Blueberry Ice Cream

There's a reason blueberries are so popular in the US, aside from their delicious taste. They are believed to be the richest source of antioxidants per pound in the fruit family and can be identified by their dark, blue-purple colour. It's often very easy to lose their delicious flavour when combining them with ice cream, as the rich dairy flavour can often overpower the fruit. So in this recipe I've added a small amount of lemon juice to bring it out.

1 large organic egg
150g Fairtrade caster sugar
300g blended blueberries
Dash of lemon juice
200ml organic full-fat milk
100ml organic double cream

1. Using a hand whisk, beat the egg and sugar together in a mixing bowl. Put them in a saucepan and place it over a low heat, stirring continuously until the mixture thickens to a custard-like consistency.

❋

2. In a blender, whizz all of the blueberries, a dash of lemon and 2–3 tablespoons of water until the mixture is completely liquid.

❋

3. Combine the custard mixture with the blueberries, return the pan to the heat then add the milk and cream. Heat gently for 10–15 minutes, stirring constantly. Remove from the heat and allow to cool.

❋

4. Pour the mixture into your ice-cream maker. Follow the manufacturer's instructions and leave to churn. (Alternatively, pour the mixture into a freezer-proof container, seal it firmly with a lid and place in the freezer. Whisk after 1 hour to prevent ice crystals from forming; repeat 3 times before leaving it to set).

❋

5. Place in the freezer to let the ice cream firm up before serving.

# British Hedgerow Ice Cream

What could be more quintessentially British than the flavours found in a summer hedgerow? You can find all of the fruits used here in the countryside from July onwards. Remember: if you're heading out foraging, be responsible and take only what you need from the hedgerow.

1 large organic egg
150g Fairtrade caster sugar
450g hedgerow fruit (wild strawberries, wild raspberries, blackberries, crab apples or redcurrants)
A dash of lemon juice
250ml organic full-fat milk
250ml organic double cream

1. Using a hand whisk, beat the egg and sugar together in a mixing bowl until the mixture takes on a smooth, pale consistency.

❋

2. Put all of your British hedgerow fruit in a blender. Add a dash of lemon juice and a few teaspoons of water and purée for approximately 5 minutes, or until the mixture is completely liquid.

❋

3. Gently heat the milk and cream in a saucepan then combine with the egg mixture and stir vigorously. Mix with the fruit purée and set aside to chill in the fridge.

❋

4. Once cool, pour the mixture into your ice-cream maker. Follow the manufacturer's instructions and leave to churn. (Alternatively, pour the mixture into a freezer-proof container, seal it firmly with a lid and place in the freezer. Whisk after 1 hour to prevent ice crystals from forming; repeat 3 times before leaving it to set).

❋

5. Once ready, place in the freezer to let the ice cream firm up before serving. Serve with a generous helping of fresh fruit and double cream.

# Butterscotch Chip Ice Cream

My grandma's favourite flavour, Butterscotch Chip, has a dairy ice-cream base (see page 33) but with the addition of butterscotch. If this is foreign territory for you, then butterscotch is a very delicious, sweet type of confectionery, usually made out of brown sugar and butter, and similar to that type of fudge you have at the seaside or at Christmas time.

100g softened butter
100g Fairtrade dark muscovado sugar
200ml organic double cream
350ml organic full-fat milk
3 large organic eggs

1. Melt the butter in a saucepan. Add the muscovado sugar and a few tablespoons of water, the cream and milk and gently warm on a medium heat. Stir constantly to avoid burning the sugar.

✳

2. In a separate heatproof bowl, whisk the eggs until light and well-combined. Gently pour the hot sugar and milk mixture over the eggs and whisk before pouring back into the saucepan.

✳

3. Return to a gentle heat and continue to stir. The mixture should begin to thicken after 5–10 minutes of constant stirring on the heat. When the custard coats the back of your spoon, it's ready. Set aside to cool before placing it in the fridge to chill.

✳

4. Once chilled, pour the mixture into your ice-cream maker. Follow the manufacturer's instructions and leave to churn. (Alternatively, pour the mixture into a freezer-proof container, seal it firmly with a lid and place in the freezer. Whisk after 1 hour to prevent ice crystals from forming; repeat 3 times before leaving it to set).

# Clotted Cream Ice Cream

As a kid growing up in the early 1990s, for me, holidays were always special, especially in the summer when they were something rare to be cherished. Summer holidays always meant a week away in my granddad's caravan to the New Forest or a seaside resort in Devon. Without fail we made a trip to a special little seaside ice-cream parlour in Poole, where we always bought rich, clotted-cream ice cream with a wafer and a scoop of fresh clotted cream on top. This recipe is my tribute to those happy memories.

4 large organic egg yolks
120g Fairtrade caster sugar
50ml organic double cream
200ml fresh clotted cream
200ml organic full-fat milk

1. Using a hand whisk, mix the egg yolks and sugar together in a heatproof bowl until they form a smooth, pale paste.

✳

2. In a medium saucepan, heat the double cream, clotted cream and milk to near-boiling point, stirring continuously to avoid burning.

✳

3. Remove the cream mixture from the heat and slowly pour it over the egg mixture. Stir to combine, then return the saucepan to the heat. Heat the mixture until it is thick enough to coat the back of your spoon, then set aside to cool.

✳

4. Pour into your ice-cream maker, follow the manufacturer's instructions and leave to churn. Place in the freezer to firm up before serving. (Alternatively, pour the mixture into a freezer-proof container, seal it firmly with a lid and place in the freezer. Whisk after 1 hour to prevent ice crystals from forming; repeat 3 times before leaving it to set.)

# English Toffee Fudge

What could possibly be more reminiscent of British summer holidays at the seaside than toffee fudge? On holiday or at home, fudge is always a winner with kids and adults alike – and this ice cream is no exception! Enjoy it topped with a generous scoop of clotted cream, or even some Hot Toffee Fudge Sauce (see page 167).

400ml organic double cream
400ml organic full-fat milk
1 large organic egg yolk
300g toffee

1. Pour the cream, milk and egg yolk into a medium or large heavy-based dishwasher-friendly saucepan and heat until the mixture nears boiling point – you'll see a few bubbles begin to rise to the surface. It's important, though, to ensure the mixture doesn't boil, so keep your eyes peeled.

※

2. Break up the toffee using a toffee hammer (or pure gusto). Add the pieces to the milk and cream mixture and leave on the heat until the toffee has melted and combined – about 10-15 minutes – stirring constantly to avoid burning the mixture.

※

3. Set the mixture aside for a further 10-15 minutes to cool before pouring it into your ice-cream maker. Follow the manufacturer's instructions and leave to churn. (Alternatively, pour the mixture into a freezer-proof container, seal it firmly with a lid and place in the freezer. Whisk after 1 hour to prevent ice crystals from forming; repeat 3 times before leaving it to set.)

# Eton Mess Ice Cream

An Eton Mess has been served at Eton's annual cricket match against rival public school Winchester College for well over a century. It's simple, stylish, delicious and refreshing, so it's no surprise that it has become the epitome of a summer dessert. The 'mess' consists of fresh strawberries (or other summer fruit), crushed meringue and a lashing of double cream – a true English classic! This dish comes recommended with a large helping of sunshine and an ice-cold glass of Pimm's or a fresh pint of organic cider!

150g Fairtrade caster sugar
1 large organic egg yolk
150ml organic full-fat milk
150ml organic double cream
150g strawberries
50g raspberries
A dash of lemon juice
50g meringues, broken

1. In a bowl, mix together the sugar and egg yolk to create a thick, pale paste. Put it in a saucepan and place over a medium heat, stirring occasionally to create a custard-like consistency.

※

2. Gently stir the milk and cream into the custard and continue to heat for approximately 10-15 minutes. As the mixture thickens and becomes more custard-like, it should coat the back of your spoon.

※

3. In a blender, purée the strawberries and raspberries with a dash of lemon juice and a few tablespoons of water. Stir the puréed fruit mixture into the custard and heat gently for a further 10 minutes to allow the flavours to infuse. Stir constantly to avoid burning. Remove the mixture from the heat and allow it to cool.

※

4. Mix in the broken meringue pieces before pouring into your ice-cream maker. Follow the manufacturer's instructions and leave to churn. (Alternatively, pour the mixture into a freezer-proof container, seal it firmly with a lid and place in the freezer. Whisk after 1 hour to prevent ice crystals from forming; repeat 3 times before leaving it to set.)

# Rhubarb Ice Cream

Although rhubarb is seasonal, it is possible to cultivate all year round – in a greenhouse, for instance. This rich-pink plant, normally considered a vegetable, is a member of the *Polygonaceae* family. Impress your friends at your next dinner party with this simple-to-make, modern ice-cream take on the British classic – or if you're home alone, then it makes great comfort food.

350g fresh rhubarb
50ml water
150g Fairtrade caster sugar
4 large organic egg yolks
300ml organic full-fat milk
250ml organic double cream

1. Roughly chop the rhubarb and put it, the water and 50g of the caster sugar in a saucepan over a medium heat. Stir well, cover and cook for up to 15 minutes, allowing the rhubarb to reduce to a thick liquid.

❋

2. In a heatproof mixing bowl, whisk together the egg yolks and the remaining 100g of sugar until you have a pale mixture with a smooth consistency.

❋

3. In a separate saucepan, bring the milk and double cream first to a simmer and then to boiling point, stirring constantly. Immediately pour it over the egg and sugar mixture and whisk thoroughly until the mixture is smooth and well-combined.

❋

4. Return the mixture to a clean saucepan and cook over a low to medium heat for 2–3 minutes, or until it's thick enough to coat the back of a spoon.

❋

5. Add the softened rhubarb and stir into the custard until fully combined. Set aside to cool before transferring the mixture to an ice-cream maker. Follow the manufacturer's instructions and leave to churn. (Alternatively, pour the mixture into a freezer-proof container, seal it firmly with a lid and place in the freezer. Whisk after 1 hour to prevent ice crystals from forming; repeat 3 times before leaving it to set.)

# Honey Ice Cream

We can, of course, thank bees for the delicious sugary nectar that makes this ice cream so delicious and smooth. Because honey is such a sweet flavour, it's easy for it to get lost in the mix of dairy, eggs and sugar that make up the custard base. To counteract this, search for orange-blossom honey, preferably from a local source. Note that I've also reduced the amount of caster sugar in this recipe, since natural sugars can be found in abundance in the honey.

300ml organic double cream
250ml organic full-fat milk
4 large organic egg yolks
100g Fairtrade caster sugar
100g local honey

1. Pour the cream and milk into a medium dishwasher-friendly saucepan and gently heat the mixture until it almost boils; you'll see a few bubbles rise to the surface. It's important, though, to ensure that it doesn't burn, so remember to stir constantly.

✳

2. Put the egg yolks into a mixing bowl with the sugar and beat with an electric whisk for about 2 minutes, until the mixture becomes a smooth paste. Put into another saucepan, place on the heat and begin to warm gently.

✳

3. Pour the milk mixture into the egg mixture, mix well, then return to the heat. Pour the honey into the custard and stir vigorously to combine. Continue to heat for approximately 10 minutes, then set aside to cool.

✳

4. Pour the custard into your ice-cream maker. Follow the manufacturer's instructions and leave to churn. (Alternatively, pour the mixture into a freezer-proof container, seal it firmly with a lid and place in the freezer. Whisk after 1 hour to prevent ice crystals from forming; repeat 3 times before leaving it to set.)

✳

5. Serve with fresh fruit or a hot toffee sauce such as the one on page 167.

# Gooseberry Fool Ice Cream

Your local fruit farm or farmers' market should stock fresh, ripe gooseberries from early August: perfect for making this smooth, timeless dessert classic into ice cream! A traditional gooseberry fool is simply crushed fruits folded into whipped cream – great on a hot summer's day. If you want to give the mixture a slightly rougher texture, just crush the cooked berries with a fork rather than sieving them. The seeds add an important contrast to the general creaminess, which helps make this the perfect companion to an ice-cold glass of Pimm's.

1 large organic egg
150g Fairtrade caster sugar
300g blended gooseberries
Dash of lemon juice
100ml organic double cream
150ml organic full-fat milk

1. Beat the egg and sugar in a mixing bowl, using a hand whisk. Pour the mixture into a saucepan and place over a medium heat, stirring constantly to avoid burning.

✳

2. In a blender, whizz up all of your gooseberries with a dash of lemon juice, until the mixture is a completely liquid purée.

✳

3. Add the purée to the egg mixture, return it to the heat, then add the milk and cream and stir well. Heat the mixture until it begins to thicken; it should coat the back of your spoon. Set aside to cool before transferring the mixture to an ice-cream maker.

✳

4. Follow the manufacturer's instructions and leave to churn. (Alternatively, pour the mixture into a freezer-proof container, seal it firmly with a lid and place in the freezer. Whisk after 1 hour to prevent ice crystals from forming; repeat 3 times before leaving it to set.)

# Lavender Ice Cream

My mother is a keen plantswoman and keeps a beautiful garden, full of colour, wild flowers and fragrant herbs. Often we have a surfeit of lavender blooms, so instead of doing nothing with them, I've found that lavender can make for a beautiful ice cream. The flavour is very delicate, but be careful of how much you use: there's a fine line between creating an aromatic ice cream and just overpowering the mixture.

250ml organic double cream
250ml organic full-fat milk
125g Fairtrade caster sugar
6 lavender stems
5 large organic egg yolks
Dash of lemon juice

1. Pour the cream and milk into a medium or large heavy-based dishwasher-friendly pan. Tip in half the sugar and the lavender stems. Allow them to soak and infuse for up to 1 hour, then place the pan over a low heat, stirring at regular intervals. Don't allow the mixture to boil.

✳

2. Whisk the egg yolks and the remaining sugar in a mixing bowl, beating with an electric whisk for about 2 minutes, or until the mixture is thick like custard.

✳

3. Add the egg mixture to the lavender mixture and stir well. Return the pan to a low heat and cook, stirring all the time, for approximately 10 minutes, until the mixture takes on a thick, custard-like consistency. Make sure it doesn't boil; as soon as you see any bubbles about to burst to the surface, it should be thick enough, so take the pan off of the heat to avoid curdling. Set aside to cool.

✳

4. Scoop out the lavender stems and pour into your ice-cream maker. Follow the manufacturer's instructions and leave to churn. (Alternatively, pour the mixture into a freezer-proof container, seal it firmly with a lid and place in the freezer. Whisk after 1 hour to prevent ice crystals from forming; repeat 3 times before leaving it to set.)

✳

5. When it has finished churning, it will probably be too soft to eat, so spoon it into a freezer-safe container and put in the freezer to firm up. Remove from the freezer 15 minutes before serving to soften slightly.

# Raspberry Ice Cream

Wild raspberries are ripe for the picking from late July onwards, but if you don't have access to wild ones, bought will do. This recipe makes just under a litre of sweet, sharp and crimson-coloured raspberry ice cream. Whether wild or cultivated, fresh raspberries are full of flavour and healthy antioxidants and are a true British summer fruit. Feel free to replace the raspberries with wild dewberries if you're looking to try something different.

300g raspberries
3 tbsp fresh lemon juice
150g Fairtrade caster sugar
200ml organic full-fat milk
100ml organic double cream
2 large organic eggs

1. Put the raspberries, lemon juice, sugar and milk in a blender and blend until you have a smooth liquid.

✳

2. In a medium saucepan, heat the cream. Add the eggs, sugar and the raspberry mixture and stir to combine over a medium heat. Be careful not to let the mixture boil; that way you avoid curdling the cream and separating the eggs. Continue to heat the mixture until it begins to thicken. Once thick enough to coat the back of a spoon, remove from the heat and set aside to cool.

✳

3. Chill in the refrigerator before pouring it into your ice-cream maker. Follow the manufacturer's instructions and leave to churn. (Alternatively, pour the mixture into a freezer-proof container, seal it firmly with a lid and place in the freezer. Whisk after 1 hour to prevent ice crystals from forming; repeat 3 times before leaving it to set.) When it has finished churning, put it in the freezer to firm up.

✳

4. Remove from the freezer 15 minutes before serving to soften slightly.

# Autumn Flavours

The autumnal transition from the end of September creates not only a patchwork of different-coloured leaves and grasses in our countryside, it also offers some interesting fresh produce. At this time, choices run from plums and damsons to a wealth of different apple varieties that heralds the start of the cider season – which is why autumn is one of my favourite times of year.

Front lawns and meadows get their last cut before the winter frost comes, and the leaf-lined streets in suburbia and national arboretums, such as Westonbirt in Gloucestershire, are awash with rich shades of brown, red, green and yellow.

The weather may have turned cooler, but that shouldn't stop you from enjoying brilliant and exciting fresh food and flavour. We all like warming fruit crumbles, for example, and ice cream complements crumble beautifully. So, when the weather turns chilly, enjoy making the most of glorious autumn fruit and vegetables. In this chapter I reveal some of my all-time favourite ice-cream recipes, including Apple & Cinnamon, Damson, Spiced Plum, and Cider & Spice ice creams. The use of cinnamon, nutmeg and star anise is very much encouraged!

*All recipes in this chapter are designed to serve 4–6 people – generously!*

CHEF'S TIP

Autumn fruit

*Apples, damsons, figs, pears, plums, sloes and late raspberries all help usher in the cider season, so make use of the delicious fruits available now. And remember: don't be afraid to experiment.*

# Apple & Cinnamon Ice Cream

This is a cool-weather favourite of mine, and pairs sweet, delicate apples with the warm, aromatic flavours of cinnamon to create a well-balanced, full-bodied ice cream reminiscent of India and the East, and said to be age-old. For best results, use freshly picked, well-ripened apples and serve with Hot Toffee Fudge Sauce (see page 167).

100g Fairtrade caster sugar
6 large organic egg yolks
250ml organic full-fat milk
300ml organic double cream
2 tsp ground cinnamon
4 large apples, peeled, cored and sliced

1. In a mixing bowl, whisk together the sugar and egg yolks to create a thick paste. Transfer this to a saucepan, then place over a medium heat, stirring occasionally to create a custard-like mixture.

❋

2. Gently stir in the milk and cream and continue to heat for approximately 10–15 minutes. As the mixture thickens and becomes more custard-like, stir in the cinnamon. Leave on the heat for a further 10 minutes to allow the flavours to infuse.

❋

3. Put the apples in a blender and blend them with a couple of tablespoons of water; continue until you have a smooth purée. If you don't have a blender, reduce the apples in a saucepan with a knob of butter and mix until they are soft and puréed.

❋

4. Combine the apple puree with the ice-cream custard and heat for approximately 5 minutes, gently stirring to ensure the mixture is fully combined.

❋

5. Remove the pan from the heat and allow the custard to cool before pouring it into your ice-cream maker. Follow the manufacturer's instructions and leave to churn. (Alternatively, pour the mixture into a freezer-proof container, seal it firmly with a lid and place in the freezer. Whisk after 1 hour to prevent ice crystals from forming; repeat 3 times before leaving it to set).

❋

6. Place in the freezer to let the ice cream set before serving.

# Crab Apple & Elderflower Ice Cream

A variety of delicious apples ripen in October, and wild crab apples
are no exception. I prefer crab apples in this recipe because their sourness
perfectly complements the sweetness of the elderflower cordial. For the cordial
I recommend either Belvoir or Bottlegreen, both of which are delicious and
of similar price and sugar content.

300ml organic full-fat milk
300ml organic double cream
3 tbsp elderflower cordial
4 large organic egg yolks
150g Fairtrade caster sugar
350g sliced crab apples
1 tsp lemon juice

1. Put the milk, cream and elderflower cordial in a saucepan and bring
to the boil. Remove from the heat and leave the flavours to infuse for
up to 10 minutes.

※

2. In a separate saucepan, whisk together the egg yolks and sugar until
the mixture is pale and smooth. Then whisk in the elderflower cream
and return the mixture to a very low heat, stirring all the time, until it
thickens and coats the back of your spoon.

※

3. Put the apple slices into a saucepan, add the lemon juice and a few
more teaspoons of elderflower cordial and cook over a low heat until
soft. Mash and leave to cool.

※

4. Add the apple mash to the custard mix and return to the heat for a further
5–10 minutes to allow the flavours to infuse before setting aside to cool.

※

5. Pour the mixture into your ice-cream maker. Follow the manufacturer's
instructions and leave to churn. (Alternatively, pour the mixture into a freezer-
proof container, seal it firmly with a lid and place in the freezer. Whisk after 1 hour
to prevent ice crystals from forming; repeat 3 times before leaving it to set).

※

6. Place in the freezer to let the ice cream set before serving. Serve with Hot
Toffee Fudge Sauce (page 167) or fruit coulis.

# Sweet Apple Ice Cream

With its contrast of crunchy crumble and sweet, soft fruit, apple crumble is an all-time classic, and one of my favourite desserts. There is just something very homely and warming about apple crumble; perhaps it's because my nan always makes us a big bowl when the apples on the trees in her garden become ripe... This recipe yields around a litre of ice cream and should take you no more than half an hour to prepare: simple, sweet and smooth. Enjoy!

About 10 large apples (I use a mix of home-grown green and red ones);
you want enough to make 300g of apple purée
A dash of lemon juice
500ml organic double cream
50g Fairtrade caster sugar
1 large organic egg

1. Wash, peel and core the apples. Use a blender to purée them with the lemon juice (plus a dash of water). If you don't have a blender, then make the purée by putting the apples into a saucepan, adding the lemon juice and cooking over a low heat until soft. Pass them through a fine-mesh sieve and set aside to cool.

❋

2. Stir the cream, sugar and egg into the purée, return the pan to the heat and heat until the sugar has completely dissolved and the mixture begins to thicken. This should take no more than 15 minutes. Stir continuously to avoid burning.

❋

3. Set the mixture aside to cool, then pour it into your ice-cream maker. Follow the manufacturer's instructions and leave to churn. (Alternatively, pour the mixture into a freezer-proof container, seal it firmly with a lid and place in the freezer. Whisk after 1 hour to prevent ice crystals from forming; repeat 3 times before leaving it to set).

❋

4. Place in the freezer to let the ice cream set before serving. Serve with a sweet fruit coulis or in a meringue nest with Hot Toffee Fudge Sauce (page 167).

## CHEF'S TIP
### Leftover fruit
*Don't throw away any leftover apples you might have lurking in the fruit bowl. Instead, turn to page 177 to find out how to make a delicious Apple & Elderflower Smoothie.*

# Cider & Spice Ice Cream

The ancient tradition of wassailing is native to Britain and was most likely first performed in the cider-growing counties of England (Gloucestershire, Worcestershire and Somerset). The ritual originally took place at the end of harvest season and was performed to help bring in a good crop by 'waking the trees' and scaring evil spirits away. The drink produced and consumed during wassailing is a very special and delicious type of hot, mulled cider, which is the inspiration for this recipe. So once made, sit back with a bowlful, contemplate life and hope for your own good harvest!

300ml organic full-fat milk
220g Fairtrade caster sugar
3 large organic egg yolks
2 tbsp ground cinnamon
250ml organic double cream
100ml organic sweet apple cider (or perry, if you prefer the flavour of pears)

1. In a saucepan, heat the milk and half of the caster sugar until just boiling. Stir continuously to avoid burning the milk. Once the mixture begins to boil, remove the saucepan from the heat.

❋

2. In a separate saucepan, whisk the egg yolks and remaining sugar until it becomes a smooth paste, then slowly pour in the hot milk and ground cinnamon, whisking until well-combined.

❋

3. Return the mixture to the saucepan and cook over a low heat until it begins to thicken. When it coats the back of a spoon, it's ready.

4. Stir in the double cream and cider and set aside to cool before pouring into your ice-cream maker.

❋

5. Follow the manufacturer's instructions and leave to churn. (Alternatively, pour the mixture into a freezer-proof container, seal it firmly with a lid and place in the freezer. Whisk after 1 hour to prevent ice crystals from forming; repeat 3 times before leaving it to set).

❋

6. Place in the freezer to let the ice cream set before serving.

# Cherry Plum Ice Cream

This delicious recipe uses wild cherry plums, which can be found in the countryside from the end of September right through to the end of autumn. Feel free to add more nutmeg to give the dish a fuller, more complex flavour.

3 large organic egg yolks
150g Fairtrade caster sugar
200ml organic full-fat milk
100ml organic double cream
400g blended fresh cherry plums
A dash of lemon juice
1 tsp nutmeg

1. Using a hand whisk, beat the egg yolks and sugar in a heatproof mixing bowl, transfer to a saucepan and place over a low heat. Stir continuously until the mixture thickens to a custard-like substance, then add the milk and cream.

❄

2. Put the cherry plums in a blender, add a dash of lemon juice and a few tablespoons of water and blend until you have a completely smooth liquid.

❄

3. Combine the custard with your plum mixture and return the pan to the heat. Stir in the nutmeg to taste and heat for 10–15 minutes, stirring constantly, until the custard begins to thicken. Remove from the heat and set aside to cool before pouring into your ice-cream maker.

❄

4. Follow the manufacturer's instructions and leave to churn. (Alternatively, pour the mixture into a freezer-proof container, seal it firmly with a lid and place in the freezer. Whisk after 1 hour to prevent ice crystals from forming; repeat 3 times before leaving it to set). Place in the freezer to let the ice cream set before serving.

# Spiced Cherry Plum Ice Cream

When I began making Cherry Plum Ice Cream, I discovered that the fruit's subtle flavour can often be lost in the ice-cream mixture, so I started looking for something to bring it out and add body. My father suggested a dash of lemon juice and a teaspoon of cinnamon. Bingo! This spiced plum recipe makes for a perfect autumn or winter ice cream. It's full of body, the warm spice of cinnamon and the subtle, delicious flavour of cherry plums.

3 large organic egg yolks
150g Fairtrade caster sugar
200ml organic full-fat milk
100ml organic double cream
400g blended fresh cherry plums
A dash of lemon juice
1 tsp cinnamon

1. In a mixing bowl, use a hand whisk to beat the egg yolks and sugar together; transfer to a saucepan and place over a low heat. Stir continuously until the mixture thickens to a custard-like consistency, then add the milk and cream.

❋

2. Put the plums in a blender, add a dash of lemon juice and a few tablespoons of water, and blend until the mixture is a completely smooth liquid.

❋

3. Combine the custard with your plum mixture and return it to the heat. Stir the cinnamon into the mixture and heat it for 10-15 minutes, stirring constantly, until it has thickened. Remove from the heat, and set aside to cool before pouring the into your ice-cream maker.

❋

4. Follow the manufacturer's instructions and leave to churn. To make by hand: follow the instructions as above, but don't add the cream with the milk; instead, whip the cream so that it's light and floppy (not too stiff), and fold it into the cold custard. Put into a freezer-proof container, seal it, and freeze for 3–4 hours, stirring once an hour until almost frozen, before leaving to freeze.

# Damson Ice Cream

Damsons are usually ripe and ready to pick from around the end of September in the UK, but they are often available through early November, depending on weather conditions. Damsons are a favourite of foragers and can be found growing near hedgerows and forests. They have a full-bodied but mellow flavour that's just perfect for ice cream, crumble and fruit pies. Leftover damsons can be baked alongside apples in a delicious crumble, or used in place of plums to make delicious smoothies.

250ml organic double cream
150ml organic full-fat milk
150g Fairtrade caster sugar
4 large organic eggs
300g blended damsons
3 tbsp water
A dash of lemon juice

1. In a mixing bowl, use a hand whisk to beat the eggs and sugar together until a pale paste has been formed. Transfer to a medium-sized saucepan and place over a low heat, stirring every few minutes to ensure the mixture doesn't burn.

❊

2. Rinse your damsons under a cold tap and use a sharp knife to remove their stones. Put the fruit together with a few tablespoons of water into a blender, whizz, then add a dash of lemon and blend again until the mixture is puréed.

❊

3. Pour the damson purée into the custard mixture and stir. Stir in the milk and cream and heat gently until the mixture thickens. Remove from the heat and set aside to cool, then chill in the fridge before pouring the mixture into your ice-cream maker.

❊

4. Follow the manufacturer's instructions and leave to churn. (Alternatively, pour the mixture into a freezer-proof container, seal it firmly with a lid and place in the freezer. Whisk after 1 hour to prevent ice crystals from forming; repeat 3 times before leaving it to set).

❊

5. Place in the freezer to let the ice cream set before serving.

# Winter Flavours

Let's face it: there's no better way to warm the heart in winter than by sharing good meals and nights of endless conversation and celebration with friends and family. Winter is a very special time of year for me, not only because of the Christmas holiday celebrations, but also due to the sheer number of family birthdays that fall between Christmas and New Year. These prove quite expensive – and with all that celebrating, very tiring!

During this time of year I can be found spending quality time with friends and loved ones, be it sat around the dinner table or slumped out in front of the fire during the long, dark evenings. In the kitchen, I use some fantastic 'winter ingredients' to create delicious, opulent ice-cream flavours, including Baileys, Chocolate Brownie, and even Christmas Pudding: all are sure to tease and excite your taste buds during the colder months and Christmas season.

*All recipes in this chapter are designed to serve 4–6 people – generously!*

## CHEF'S TIP
### Winter flavours
*Replenish your spice rack and store cupboard by visiting your local specialist food store for nutmeg, allspice, mixed spice, cinnamon, star anise, high-quality cocoa and dark spirits. Really get into the festive spirit by experimenting with fragrant, warming flavours such as Apple & Cinnamon and Clove Ice Cream – or even my take on Indian kulfi.*

# Baileys Ice Cream

It's no surprise that Baileys is one of the best-selling spirits in the UK at Christmas time. If you're not familiar with this alcoholic favourite, then it can only be described as creamy, rich and silky-smooth. As an addition to ice cream, it makes a perfect winter warmer. Be aware, though, that its added alcohol content means that you need to be conservative with your measurements. As with all alcohol-based ice creams, leave the mixture to freeze overnight in order for it to harden, ready for serving.

250ml organic double cream
250ml organic full-fat milk
100g Fairtrade caster sugar
75ml Baileys Irish Cream

1. Put the cream, milk and sugar in a medium saucepan over a medium heat. Stir continuously to combine, and heat until the mixture reaches boiling point.

※

2. Slowly pour the Baileys into the hot mixture, stir well and put over a low heat for up to 10 minutes, until the mixture has thickened. Set aside to cool, then put in the fridge to chill.

※

3. Pour the mixture into your ice-cream maker. Follow the manufacturer's instructions and leave to churn. (Alternatively, pour the mixture into a freezer-proof container, seal it firmly with a lid and place in the freezer. Whisk after 1 hour to prevent ice crystals from forming; repeat 3 times before leaving it to set).

※

4. Once churning is complete, transfer the ice cream into a freezer-friendly container and freeze overnight. Serve with a splash of Baileys over the top.

# Brown Bread Ice Cream

This recipe is thought to date back to the Victorian era, when ice cream was a treat reserved for the rich. It makes use of caramelised scraps of brown bread to produce a sweet and somewhat subtle flavour, with the addition of brown sugar – simple and delicious. To make it, I've used organic brown bread from Tom Herbert's Hobbs House Bakery.

50g brown breadcrumbs
150g Fairtrade brown caster sugar
150ml organic full-fat milk
350ml organic double cream
1 tsp Madagascar bourbon vanilla extract
A dash of lemon juice

1. Put the breadcrumbs on a baking tray and sprinkle with the sugar, spreading out all of the breadcrumbs evenly and ensuring an even coverage of sugar. Place the tray under a grill on a medium heat, checking constantly to see that the breadcrumbs don't burn.

※

2. Keep spreading out the breadcrumbs and returning them to the heat until both the sugar and breadcrumbs have caramelised. Remove from the heat and set aside to cool slightly.

※

3. Before the breadcrumb-caramel mixture has completely cooled, put it in a bowl, add the milk and double cream and stir vigorously.

※

4. Pour the mixture into a medium, heavy-based saucepan, stir in the vanilla extract and lemon juice, then place over a medium heat for approximately 10 minutes. Set aside to cool.

※

5. Pour into your ice-cream maker. Follow the manufacturer's instructions and leave to churn. (Alternatively, pour the mixture into a freezer-proof container, seal it firmly with a lid and place in the freezer. Whisk after 1 hour to prevent ice crystals from forming; repeat 3 times before leaving it to set).

※

6. Place in the freezer to let the ice cream set before serving.

# Chocolate Brownie Ice Cream

While working on this book I spent a lot of time writing or brainstorming in coffee shops, and also milling around my kitchen developing new recipes. This resulted in my Coffee & Cream recipe on page 110 and also this Chocolate Brownie recipe. If you haven't got time to bake your own brownies, then I recommend 7aCoffeeShop or Blue Basil Brownies. Both are based in the Cotswolds and are famous for their delicious brownies. This recipe is pure chocolate heaven and makes the perfect comfort food for those cold winter nights.

200ml organic double cream
200ml organic full-fat milk
150g Fairtrade caster sugar
80g chocolate (at least 70%), roughly chopped
1 large organic egg yolk
100g diced chocolate brownie

1. Pour the cream and milk into a medium or large heavy-based dishwasher-friendly saucepan. Tip in half the sugar and all the chocolate and place over a low heat, stirring at regular intervals. You want to allow the chocolate to melt but not boil or burn.

❄

2. Whisk the egg yolk and the remaining sugar in a mixing bowl, beating with an electric whisk for about 2 minutes, or until the mixture has thickened.

❄

3. Combine both mixtures and return the pan to a low heat. Cook, stirring all the time, for approximately 10 minutes, until the mixture takes on a thick, custard-like consistency. Be careful that it doesn't boil; as soon as you see any bubbles about to burst to the surface, it should be thick enough, so take the pan off of the heat to prevent curdling and leave it to cool.

❄

4. Stir in the diced brownie, then pour the mixture into your ice-cream maker and follow the manufacturer's instructions and leave to churn. (Alternatively, pour the mixture into a freezer-proof container, seal it firmly with a lid and place in the freezer. Whisk after 1 hour to prevent ice crystals from forming; repeat 3 times before leaving it to set). While waiting, sit back and enjoy life.

❄

5. Once the churning is complete, put the ice cream in the freezer for an hour to set before serving.

# Aztec Gold

This delicious and extraordinarily decadent recipe was once favoured by high society, and became the centrepiece of countless dinner-party and banquet tables. It uses high-quality cocoa (which is full of flavour notes), rich cream and organic milk, topped with a lavish embellishment of gold leaf. To create a truly dramatic display, consider putting the ice cream into moulds before freezing.

4 large organic egg yolks
150g Fairtrade caster sugar
200ml organic double cream
50ml dark rum
1 tsp rum flavouring
200ml organic full-fat milk
50g organic raisins

1. Put the egg yolks and sugar into a heatproof mixing bowl and beat with an electric whisk for about 2 minutes, until the mixture has thickened and falls in thick ribbons. Beat in the cream.

❋

2. In a saucepan combine the rum, rum flavouring and milk and heat for up to 15 minutes, bringing the mixture close to the boil.

❋

3. Pour the milk mixture over the egg mixture, stir to combine, then put back into the saucepan and return to a low heat. Heat, stirring, until the mixture begins to thicken to a custard-like consistency. If it coats the back of a spoon, it should be thick enough, so remove the pan from the heat and set aside to cool.

❋

4. Pour into your ice-cream maker, follow the manufacturer's instructions and leave to churn. (Alternatively, pour the mixture into a freezer-proof container, seal it firmly with a lid and place in the freezer. Whisk after 1 hour to prevent ice crystals from forming; repeat 3 times before leaving it to set.)

❋

5. Serve with a generous scoop of clotted cream and decorate with edible gold leaf.

# Honey & Spéculoos Ice Cream

This recipe was suggested by a close friend who spent more than a year living and studying in the south of France. Spéculoos (German *Spekulatius* or Dutch *Speculaas*) are sweet, golden biscuits made with spices – cinnamon, nutmeg, clove, ginger and cardamom. As their many names suggest, they're popular in France, Germany and Belgium, and I love using them to make this ice cream. Here the sweet addition of orange-blossom honey means that less raw caster sugar is needed; mine comes from the delicious Gusto Deli in Cheltenham.

300ml organic double cream
300ml organic full-fat milk
4 large organic egg yolks
100g Fairtrade caster sugar
100g local honey
50g crushed spéculoos

1. Pour the cream and milk into a medium dishwasher-friendly saucepan and heat gently until the mixture almost boils; you'll see a few bubbles begin to surface. Stir constantly to ensure it doesn't burn.

✳

2. Put the egg yolks and sugar in a heatproof mixing bowl and beat with an electric whisk for about 2 minutes, until the mixture becomes a smooth paste. Put into another saucepan, place on the heat and begin to warm gently.

✳

3. Pour the milk mixture into the egg mixture, mix well then return to the heat. Add the honey and spéculoos and stir vigorously to combine. Heat for approximately 10 minutes, set aside to cool, then put the ice-cream mixture into the fridge to chill.

✳

4. Pour the custard into your ice-cream maker. Follow the manufacturer's instructions and leave to churn. (Alternatively, pour the mixture into a freezer-proof container, seal it firmly with a lid and place in the freezer. Whisk after 1 hour to prevent ice crystals from forming; repeat 3 times before leaving it to set.)

✳

5. Serve with fresh fruit or Hot Toffee Fudge Sauce (page 167).

# Christmas Pudding Ice Cream

This recipe never fails to impress friends and family at Christmas time. It's full of pungent winter spices and a rich collection of fruit, but it's really simple and quick to make. Here I advise decanting the ice-cream mixture into a pudding bowl, freezing it and turning it out when ready to serve. Not only will the ice cream look and taste just like a real Christmas pudding, it will act as a good alternative for those who find the richness of Christmas pudding too much.

1 tsp mixed spice
1 tsp ground clove
4 tbsp quality brandy
300g organic dried fruit
150ml full-fat milk
150ml organic double cream
50g full-fat natural yoghurt
2 tbsp local honey

1. In a bowl, combine the spices and the brandy. Leave covered in a cool, dry place for approximately half an hour to allow the flavours to infuse.

\*

2. Pour the brandy-based liquid over the dried fruit and leave to soak and infuse for an hour or so, covered, in a cool, dry place.

\*

3. Combine the milk, cream, yoghurt and honey with the infused fruit mixture, ensuring that all of the fruit is adequately mixed.

\*

4. Pour the mixture into your ice-cream maker. Follow the manufacturer's instructions and leave to churn. (Alternatively, pour the mixture into a freezer-proof container, seal it firmly with a lid and place in the freezer. Whisk after 1 hour to prevent ice crystals from forming; repeat 3 times before leaving it to set.)

# Rice Pudding Ice Cream

Surprisingly, rice pudding is eaten in various forms around the world. It's thought to have emerged in Britain during the Tudor period. This ice cream is an ode to the great British dish, and can be served lovingly with a generous scoop of strawberry jam or golden syrup. Note: If you don't have time to make the Traditional Vanilla Ice Cream recipe listed on page 30, then I would of course recommend using Winstones Cotswold Ice Cream, available from various delis, grocers, ice-cream parlours and selected Waitrose and the Co-op stores. Note: you really do need an ice-cream maker for this recipe to aerate it properly and achieve the desired consistency.

Ingredients
500ml organic full-fat milk
15g unsalted butter, softened
50g Fairtrade caster sugar
50g short-grain pudding rice
500ml Traditional Vanilla Ice Cream (see page 30)

1. Put the milk, butter and sugar in a saucepan and bring to the boil. Add the rice and bring to a simmer. Cook gently for up to 30 minutes, stirring frequently, until the rice becomes soft and the water content reduces. Set aside and leave to cool completely.

✳

2. Mix the rice with the ice cream, pour into your ice-cream maker and churn for 15–20 minutes until thickened and increased in volume. Transfer to a freezer-friendly container, cover with a lid or cling film and leave to freeze overnight.

✳

3. Remove from the freezer and leave to soften for 15 minutes before serving.

# Clove Ice Cream

Clove is traditionally used in Indian cuisine and Christmas cookery,
thanks largely to its aromatic and pungent flavouring. Here I have used
two rather conservative teaspoons of ground cloves, which produces
a flavoursome ice cream. The trick is to balance the amount of clove used;
you don't want to lose the aromatic flavour in the mixture but you
must also be careful not to overpower the ice cream.

100g Fairtrade caster sugar
6 large organic egg yolks
250ml organic full-fat milk
400ml organic double cream
2 tsp ground cloves

1. In a bowl, mix the sugar and egg yolks together to create a thick paste.
Transfer to a saucepan and put over a medium heat, stirring occasionally
to create a custard-like consistency.

*

2. Gently stir in the milk and cream and continue to heat for approximately
10–15 minutes. As the mixture thickens and becomes more custard-like,
stir in the ground cloves. Leave on the heat for a further 10 minutes
to allow the flavours to infuse. Remove the mixture from the heat and
allow it to cool before pouring into your ice-cream maker.

*

3. Follow the manufacturer's instructions and leave to churn.
(Alternatively pour the mixture into a freezer-proof container, place at
the back of the freezer and remove after 1 hour and whisk; repeat 3 times
before leaving to set.)

*

4. Serve with a generous helping of double cream.

# Dark Chocolate Ice Cream

A rich, full-bodied 85 per cent cocoa will create a deliciously devilish ice cream full of rich chocolate flavour notes. Simple to make, this one is complemented perfectly with a large scoop of clotted cream – or even vanilla ice cream.

200ml organic double cream
200ml organic full-fat milk
150g Fairtrade caster sugar
100g chocolate (at least 85% cocoa solids), roughly chopped
1 large organic egg yolk

1. Pour the cream and milk into a saucepan. Add half of the sugar and all of the chocolate and place over a low heat, stirring at regular intervals, allowing the chocolate to melt but not boil or burn.

✳

2. Whisk the egg yolk and the remaining sugar in a mixing bowl, beating with an electric whisk for about 2 minutes, or until the mixture has thickened to a smooth, custard-like consistency.

✳

3. Combine both custard and chocolate mixtures and return the pan to a low heat. Continue to heat the custard gently for approximately 10 minutes, or until the mixture is thick enough to coat the back of a spoon. Remove from the heat and set aside to cool.

✳

4. Pour the cooled mixture into your ice-cream maker, follow the manufacturer's instructions and leave to churn. (Alternatively, pour the mixture into a freezer-proof container, seal with a tight-fitting lid, and place at the back of the freezer. Remove after 1 hour and whisk; repeat 3 times before leaving to set solid.)

✳

5. Once the ice-cream maker has finished churning, put the ice cream into the freezer for a further half-hour before serving with a generous scoop of clotted cream.

# Guinness Ice Cream

Surprisingly, the smooth, creamy Irish 'black gold' known as Guinness makes for a perfect ice cream. In fact, while its richness suits the colder months, Guinness Ice Cream is an ideal year-round recipe: a delicious after-dinner dessert for a St Patrick's Day feast, or a great partner to virtually any red-meat dish. I've decided to place this recipe in the winter season, though, because Guinness itself is dark and rich and often drunk during the holiday season.

3 large organic egg yolks
50g Fairtrade caster sugar
250ml organic full-fat milk
250ml organic double cream
200ml Guinness

1. Whisk the egg yolks and sugar in a mixing bowl, beating with an electric whisk for about 2 minutes, or until the mixture forms a light, pale, smooth paste. Pour into a saucepan and heat gently, stirring occasionally to prevent burning.

✳

2. In a separate saucepan, gently begin to heat the milk and cream, but stir constantly to avoid bringing to the boil. Slowly pour the Guinness into the milk mixture and stir vigorously for up to 5 minutes to ensure all the ingredients are adequately combined.

✳

3. Combine the Guinness mixture with the egg mixture and return it to the heat. Continue to stir until fully combined and the custard begins to thicken. Remove from the heat and set aside to cool.

✳

4. Pour the mixture into your ice-cream maker, follow the manufacturer's instructions and leave to churn. (Alternatively pour the mixture into a freezer-proof container, place at the back of the freezer and remove after 1 hour and whisk; repeat 3 times before leaving to set solid.) While waiting, sit back and enjoy life.

✳

5. When ready, put the ice cream in the freezer for an hour to firm up before serving.

# Mulled Wine Ice Cream

In my house, Christmas wouldn't be Christmas without a piping-hot glass of intensely rich, aromatic homemade mulled wine. This ice cream uses cloves, red wine and mulling syrup to create an aromatic Christmas ice-cream flavour.

600ml red wine
50ml mulling syrup
2 tsp ground cloves
150g Fairtrade caster sugar
200ml double cream
6 large organic egg yolks

1. Pour the red wine, mulling syrup, ground cloves and half of the sugar into a medium saucepan. Cover and leave to simmer for 30 minutes, stirring occasionally.

✳

2. Remove the lid and gently increase the heat. Leave to simmer for another 30 minutes to allow the wine to reduce before setting aside to cool.

✳

3. In a separate saucepan, bring the cream to a simmer. In a heatproof bowl, whisk together the remaining sugar and egg yolks to a thick, smooth paste. Now pour the hot cream over the egg yolks, transfer to the saucepan and return to a low heat until the mixture thickens – enough to coat the back of your spoon. Set the mixture aside to cool.

✳

4. Mix the egg mixture with the mulled-wine mixture and place in the refrigerator to chill before pouring into your ice-cream maker. Follow the manufacturer's instructions and leave to churn, then put in the freezer to harden. (Alternatively pour the mixture into a freezer-proof container, secure with a tight-fitting lid and place at the back of the freezer. Remove after 1 hour and whisk; repeat 3 times before leaving to set solid.)

✳

5. Remove from the freezer 15 minutes before serving to soften slightly, and bingo! Happy Christmas!

# White Chocolate & Truffle Ice Cream

Personally, I've always found white chocolate sickly and far too sweet for my palate. However, due to popular demand, and having been asked to create a white chocolate ice cream recipe for my friends, I've developed this simple and easy-to-follow one based on the chocolate recipe found in the Basic Flavours chapter (see page 35). This recipe includes truffle oil, now readily available from most delis and supermarkets.

1 tbsp truffle oil
200ml organic double cream
200ml organic full-fat milk
150g Fairtrade caster sugar
80g Fairtrade white chocolate, roughly chopped
1 large organic egg yolk

1. Pour the oil, cream and milk into a medium or large dishwasher-friendly heavy-based pan. Stir in half the sugar and all the white chocolate and put over a low heat, stirring at regular intervals to allow the chocolate to melt but not boil or burn.

❊

2. In a mixing bowl, whisk the egg yolk and the remaining sugar together, beating with an electric whisk for about 2 minutes, or until the mixture has thickened like custard.

❊

3. Combine both mixtures in the saucepan and return to a low heat, stirring all the time, for approximately 10 minutes, or until the mixture takes on a thick, custard-like consistency. Make sure it doesn't boil; as soon as you see any bubbles about to burst to the surface, it should be thick enough, so take the pan off the heat and leave to cool.

❊

4. Pour into your ice-cream maker, follow the manufacturer's instructions and leave to churn. (Alternatively pour the mixture into a freezer-proof container, place at the back of the freezer and remove after 1 hour and whisk; repeat 3 times before leaving to set solid.) While waiting, sit back and enjoy life.

❊

5. When ready, put in the freezer for an hour to firm up before serving.

# All Year Round Flavours

The recipes in this chapter don't fit into a definitive seasonal category. Some are more exotic than others, made from ingredients that don't rely on locally sourced ingredients for their manufacture.

Unfortunately, to satisfy taste buds it isn't always possible to source everything locally. While I always advocate local sources for your ingredients whenever possible, we do live in a globalised world, where we have access to a rich variety of herbs, spices, fruits and flavours, from the exotic to the extraordinary. It would be a shame not to make use of them once in a while.

*All recipes in this chapter are designed to serve 4–6 people – generously!*

# Lemon Meringue Ice Cream

Without doubt, lemon is one of my favourite fruits. I have a strange affinity with it, since the first recipe I ever made was a tart au citron while staying with family in the south of France. I love the tart, fresh flavour of freshly squeezed lemon – and that's exactly what makes this a family favourite ice-cream flavour. Pieces of meringue are added for texture and taste; to make life easy, feel free to crush up some meringues from your local cake shop or farmers' market. Mine come from the fantastic Meringue Company, based in Nailsworth.

Zest of 4 large, organic lemons
250ml organic full-fat milk
4 large organic egg yolks
150g Fairtrade caster sugar
1 meringue, crushed
250ml organic double cream

1. First, infuse the lemon zest with the milk: add the lemon zest to the milk in a saucepan. Warm the mixture over a low heat until it is hot but not boiling. Remove and set aside to cool, allowing the flavours to infuse further for up to 1 hour.

❋

2. Whisk the egg yolks and sugar together in a heatproof mixing bowl until they form a smooth paste. Bring the milk mixture back to the boil and pour it into the bowl, stirring well. Return to the heat, stirring constantly, until the mixture thickens. Set aside to cool, then put in the refrigerator to chill.

❋

3. Fold in the cream, then pour the mixture into your ice-cream maker. Follow the manufacturer's instructions and leave to churn. (Alternatively, pour the mixture into a freezer-proof container, seal it firmly with a lid and place in the freezer. Whisk after 1 hour to prevent ice crystals from forming; repeat 3 times before leaving it to set.)

❋

4. When it has finished churning, your ice cream will probably be too soft to eat, so spoon it into a freezer-safe container and put in the freezer to set. Remove from the freezer 15 minutes before serving to soften slightly. Serve in a bowl with the crushed meringue and a scoop of clotted cream.

# Rum & Raisin Ice Cream

Rum is available as either a dark or light spirit, but for this classic recipe I favour the use of Havana Club Dark Rum. The combination of dark rum and delicious organic raisins adds texture and sweetness to the ice cream.

50g organic raisins
50ml dark rum
1 large organic egg yolk
150g Fairtrade caster sugar
200ml organic full-fat milk
200ml organic double cream
1 tsp rum flavouring

1. Pour the raisins into a saucepan and add the rum. Place over a medium heat to warm, and stir occasionally to allow the flavours to infuse. After 5–10 minutes, remove from the heat and set aside so that the raisins can soak up some of the rum.
✳

2. Put the egg yolk and sugar into a heatproof bowl and whisk together until they form a pale, smooth paste.
✳

3. Pour the milk into a saucepan and bring slowly to the boil. Pour the boiling milk on to the egg yolk mixture and whisk well until fully combined, then pour back into the saucepan and return to the heat. Stir continuously to avoid burning.
✳

4. Add the cream, rum, raisins and rum flavouring and continue stirring until thickened. Do not allow the mixture to boil. Remove from the heat and allow to cool
✳

5. Pour into your ice-cream machine, follow the manufacturer's instructions and leave to churn. (Alternatively pour the mixture into a freezer-proof container, place at the back of the freezer and remove after 1 hour and whisk; repeat 3 times before leaving to set.)

# Grape & Lime Ice Cream

Grape & Lime Ice Cream is full of a fresh, clean flavour that's sure to excite
your taste buds. It's one of the few ice creams I make that
break my seasonality and localism rule.

250ml organic double cream
350ml organic full-fat milk
50g Fairtrade caster sugar
100ml grape juice
A dash of lime juice

1. In a medium saucepan, combine the cream and milk and slowly
bring the mixture to the boil. Give it your full attention,
stirring constantly to avoid burning.

✳

2. Pour in the sugar and stir to combine. Continue to stir over the heat
until all of the sugar has dissolved.

✳

3. Add the grape juice and lime juice to taste and stir to combine,
then set aside to cool before placing into the refrigerator to chill.

✳

4. Once the mixture has chilled, pour it into your ice-cream maker.
Follow the manufacturer's instructions and leave to churn.
(Alternatively, pour the mixture into a freezer-proof container,
seal it firmly with a lid and place in the freezer. Whisk after 1 hour
to prevent ice crystals from forming; repeat
3 times before leaving it to set.).

# Dark Chocolate & Wild Cherry Ice Cream

If you're a fan of dark chocolate and flavourful, tangy fruit, then this is the flavour for you! Here the combination of dark chocolate and late-growing wild cherry produces a rich, dark ice cream full of bright, tangy cherry flavour. Replace the cherries with blackberries or even raspberries for variation.

200ml organic double cream
200ml organic full-fat milk
150g Fairtrade caster sugar
80g chocolate (at least 80%) roughly chopped
1 large organic egg yolk
2 tsp cherry liqueur
10–15 wild cherries, halved

1. Pour the cream and milk into a saucepan and stir in half the sugar and all of the chocolate. Place over a low heat, stirring at regular intervals and allowing the chocolate to melt but not boil or burn.

❋

2. In a mixing bowl, whisk together the egg yolk and the remaining sugar, beating with an electric whisk for about 2 minutes, or until the mixture has thickened to a smooth, custard-like consistency.

❋

3. Add the egg mixture to the chocolate mixture, pour in the cherry liqueur and cherries to taste and return the pan to a low heat. Continue to heat the custard gently for approximately 10 minutes, until the mixture is thick enough to coat the back of a spoon. Remove from the heat and set aside to cool.

❋

4. Pour the cooled mixture into your ice-cream maker, follow the manufacturer's instructions and leave to churn. (Alternatively pour the mixture into a freezer-proof container, seal with a tight-fitting lid, place at the back of the freezer and remove after 1 hour and whisk; repeat 3 times before leaving to set solid.) Sit back, switch on the radio and wait patiently.

❋

5. Once the churning is complete, put the ice cream into the freezer for a further half-hour before serving with Hot Toffee Fudge Sauce (see page 167).

# Banana & Toffee Ice Cream

Sure, banana and toffee aren't ingredients that exactly scream traditional Cotswolds, but much like Rum & Raisin (see page 103), this flavour has become a favourite with ice-cream lovers across the globe. The natural sugars in the banana and the richness of the toffee give this combination its timeless appeal. Remember to use Fairtrade bananas and top lovingly with a generous helping of Hot Toffee Fudge Sauce (see page 167) or maple syrup.

4 large Fairtrade bananas
25g Fairtrade caster sugar
1 tsp lemon juice
250ml organic full-fat milk
250ml organic double cream
200g toffee

1. Peel and chop the bananas, then put them into a blender. Add the sugar, lemon juice and a couple of tablespoons of water and blend until smooth.

✳

2. Add the milk and blend again until the ingredients are fully combined. Set aside in the refrigerator to chill.

✳

3. In a saucepan, gently heat the cream. Using a hammer or rolling pin, break up the toffee into small chunks. Add the toffee to the cream and heat until fully dissolved, stirring constantly to prevent burning. Set aside to cool.

✳

4. Add the cream-toffee to the banana mixture, then return to a low heat for a further 10-15 minutes to ensure that the banana and toffee have fully infused. Set aside to cool.

✳

5. Pour the mixture into your ice-cream maker. Follow the manufacturer's instructions and leave to churn. (Alternatively, pour the mixture into a freezer-proof container, seal it firmly with a lid and place in the freezer. Whisk after 1 hour to prevent ice crystals from forming; repeat 3 times before leaving it to set).

✳

6. Place in the freezer to let the ice cream set before serving.

# Green Tea Ice Cream

One of the greatest gifts of world trade is variety, and thanks to the sheer number of different herbs, spices, fruits and vegetables readily available, we can enjoy exciting, new flavours. One in particular is green tea, available from most good delis, tea or coffee shops and supermarkets. Matcha is, in essence, powdered green tea with a powerful flavour and even more powerful bright-green colour.

125g Fairtrade caster sugar
4 large organic egg yolks
250ml organic full-fat milk
250ml organic double cream
3 tsp matcha green tea powder
1 tsp fresh lemon juice

1. In a heatproof bowl, mix together the sugar and egg yolks to create a thick, pale paste. Put this in a saucepan and place over a medium heat, stirring occasionally to create a custard-like mixture.

*

2. Gently stir the milk and cream into the mixture, mix well, then continue to heat, stirring constantly, for approximately 10-15 minutes. As the mixture thickens and becomes more custard-like, it should coat the back of your spoon.

*

3. Stir the matcha and dash of lemon juice into the custard, then leave it to cook for a further 10 minutes to allow the flavours to infuse. Stir constantly to avoid burning.

*

4. Remove the custard from the heat, set aside to cool, then allow it to chill in the fridge before pouring into your ice-cream maker. Follow the manufacturer's instructions and leave to churn. (Alternatively, pour the mixture into a freezer-proof container, seal it firmly with a lid and place in the freezer. Whisk after 1 hour to prevent ice crystals from forming; repeat 3 times before leaving it to set.)

# Coffee & Cream Ice Cream

I've found that, much like Marmite, friends and family either love or hate coffee, but by adding a large amount of cream, it is possible to achieve a flavour that is both mild and flavoursome. Here I've used Rocket Coffee, a local supplier based just outside my hometown of Nailsworth. Entrepreneur Lee Bolam, the owner of Rocket Coffee, is committed not only to ethical practice and localism, but also to honest, Fairtrade coffee full of flavour notes. After a chance meeting, Lee suggested I try his coffee – and I was instantly hooked!

50g organic espresso/coffee beans
250ml organic double cream
350ml organic full-fat milk
4 large organic egg yolks
150g golden caster sugar

1. Using your blender, blend the coffee/espresso beans until they are completely crushed. Put them in a medium or large heavy-based dishwasher-friendly saucepan, add the cream and milk, gently heat the mixture for up to 10 minutes, then remove from the heat and leave to cool.

❄

2. In a bowl, mix the egg yolks and sugar together; beat the mixture until it becomes a smooth, light paste. Using a strainer, pour the coffee mixture into the egg mixture, stir to combine, then put it back in the saucepan and return to a medium heat.

❄

3. Whisk constantly and leave on heat for 10–15 minutes to ensure that the mixture doesn't boil. Set aside to cool.

❄

4. Pour the mixture into your ice-cream maker, follow the manufacturer's instructions and leave to churn. (Alternatively pour the mixture into a freezer-proof container, seal it with a tight-fitting lid, place it at the back of the freezer and remove after 1 hour and whisk; repeat 3 times before leaving it to set.)

# Golden Syrup Ice Cream

In 1881, Scottish businessman Abram Lyle set up a sugar refinery
on the banks of the river Thames. When he found that a gloopy, golden syrup
was created during the refining process, Lyle eventually launched it as a
product on its own – to great success. Here the rich flavour of Lyle's Golden
Syrup can easily get lost within the dairy flavour of the ice cream, so it's
important to ensure you are conservative with your milk and cream.

3 large organic egg yolks
150g Lyle's Golden Syrup
250ml organic full-fat milk
250ml organic double cream

1. In a mixing bowl, whisk the egg yolks, beating with an electric whisk
for about 2 minutes, or until light, pale and smooth. Pour into a saucepan and
heat gently, stirring occasionally to avoid burning.

✳

2. Fill a separate saucepan with water and bring it to the boil. Remove the lid
from the Golden Syrup tin, then carefully place the tin in the water for
approximately 5 minutes to make the syrup more malleable. Remove the tin
from the heat and pour the syrup into the eggs. Add the milk and cream.

✳

3. Return the mixture to the heat and continue to stir until everything
is fully combined and the mixture begins to thicken. Remove the pan
from the heat and set aside to cool.

✳

4. Pour the mixture into your ice-cream maker and follow the
manufacturer's instructions. Leave to churn. (Alternatively, pour it into
a freezer-proof container, seal it with a tight-fitting lid, place at the back
of the freezer, then remove after 1 hour and whisk; repeat 3 times before
leaving it to set.) While waiting, sit back and enjoy life.

✳

5. When the churning is complete, put the ice cream in the freezer for
an hour to firm up before serving.

# Honey & Ginger Ice Cream

This recipe is based on the Honey Ice Cream recipe on page 58, but with one exception: the addition of ginger. To save time I've used ground ginger because root ginger may be expensive and time-consuming to grate, plus it contains natural sugars that aren't needed. Ginger works well with honey to create a delicate, well-balanced flavour that's perfect all year round. Remember, because plain honey has such a subtle flavour, try to use orange-blossom honey if you can find it. I buy mine from the Gusto Deli in Cheltenham.

300ml organic double cream
2 tsp ground ginger
250ml organic full-fat milk
4 large organic egg yolks
100g Fairtrade caster sugar
100g local honey

1. Pour the cream, ginger and milk into a medium dishwasher-friendly saucepan and gently heat the mixture until it's close to boiling point; you'll see a few bubbles begin to rise to the surface. Stir constantly to ensure that the mixture doesn't burn.

✳

2. Put the egg yolks into a mixing bowl with the sugar and beat with an electric whisk for about 2 minutes, until the mixture becomes a smooth paste. Put it into another saucepan, place on the heat and begin to warm gently.

✳

3. Pour the milk mixture into the egg mixture, mix well, then return to the heat. Pour the honey into the custard and stir vigorously to combine. Heat for approximately 10 minutes. Set aside to cool, then put the ice-cream mixture into the fridge to chill.

✳

4. Pour the mixture into your ice-cream maker. Follow the manufacturer's instructions and leave to churn. (Alternatively, pour the mixture into a freezer-proof container, seal it firmly with a lid and place in the freezer. Whisk after 1 hour to prevent ice crystals from forming; repeat 3 times before leaving it to set.)

✳

5. Serve with fresh fruit or Hot Toffee Fudge Sauce (see page 167).

# Orange Marmalade Ice Cream

This is my father's all-time favourite. Seeing him enjoy marmalade spread over toast got me to thinking that marmalade ice cream might just work – and, surprise surprise, it really does! Following this recipe should give you approximately 1 litre of ice cream: enough for at least five people to have a generous portion.

250ml organic double cream
250ml organic full-fat milk
50g Fairtrade caster sugar
300g organic orange marmalade
3 tbsp fresh orange juice (or to taste)

1. Put the cream, milk, sugar and marmalade in a blender and blend, adding the orange juice to taste.

❋

2. Once the mixture has reached a liquid consistency, transfer it to a saucepan and heat for 10-15 minutes over a medium heat. Be careful not to boil it to avoid 'cream curdling'.

❋

3. Allow the mixture to cool before pouring it into your ice-cream maker. Follow the manufacturer's instructions and leave to churn. (Alternatively, pour the mixture into a freezer-proof container, seal it firmly with a lid and place it in the freezer. Whisk after 1 hour to prevent ice crystals from forming; repeat 3 times before leaving it to set.)

## CHEF'S TIP
### How to make orange marmalade
*Use 1kg of fresh oranges, 1kg of granulated white sugar and 1kg of muscovado sugar, 1 lemon (or a handful of cranberries). Juice the oranges and lemon and shred skins to create peel, put everything in a pan over a medium heat with 2 litres of water, heat for at least 2 hours, then leave to cool before transferring to 1 marmalade jar.*

# Indian Kulfi

Kulfi is traditionally Indian and has an opulent spicy/milky flavour with a number of taste variations. Indian cuisine is a particular favourite of mine, but I've always been left relatively disappointed by Indian desserts, often some sort of pre-bought frozen treat that would sit well in the 1980s. I was pleasantly surprised when I came across some delicious kulfi at a restaurant in the Parisian Latin Quarter just a few years ago, and I've been hooked ever since. Aromatic, rich and full of delicate spices, this recipe is perfect for summer or winter. Note: kulfi is difficult to make by hand, so you really do need an ice-cream maker here. Also, kulfi moulds are available from all good kitchen shops, usually for under the £5 mark. Alternatively, use a standard jelly mould.

1 tsp saffron
1 tsp cinnamon
1 tsp ground cloves
200ml full-fat milk
50ml condensed milk
250ml organic double cream
150g Fairtrade caster sugar
1 tbsp rose water

1. Combine the spices, milk and condensed milk in a saucepan and place over a medium heat for up to 10 minutes to allow the flavours to infuse. Stir occasionally to avoid burning the mixture.

※

2. Add the cream, sugar and rose water to the milk and return to the heat for 10-15 minutes, allowing the mixture to heat up but not quite boil.

※

3. Ensure that the flavour is to your liking and adjust the spices accordingly, then set the mixture aside to cool.

※

4. Pour the kulfi mixture into your ice-cream maker, but bear in mind you're after a dense, icy consistency with this one; thus the mixture will need to be churned only for about 15 minutes before pouring it into kulfi moulds and freezing.

※

5. Freeze for at least 5 hours before serving.

# Mixed Spice Ice Cream

I was asked to develop a mixed-spice ice cream by a Turkish restaurant, and quickly found that I was unable to keep up with the sheer level of demand. This recipe is my Turkish take on the Indian Kulfi recipe on the opposite page and it largely follows the Clove Ice Cream recipe from page 88.

100g Fairtrade caster sugar
6 large organic egg yolks
250ml organic full-fat milk
400ml organic double cream
2 tsp mixed spice

1. In a heatproof mixing bowl, whisk the sugar and egg yolks together to create a thick paste. Pour the milk and cream into a saucepan and heat to near-boiling point.

✳

2. Gently stir the hot milk and cream into the egg mixture, then transfer back to the saucepan and return to the heat. The mixture should begin to thicken after 10–15 minutes. As it thickens and becomes more custard-like, stir in the mixed spice. Leave on the heat for a further 10 minutes to allow the flavours to infuse.

✳

3. Remove from the heat and allow to cool before pouring into your ice-cream maker. Follow the manufacturer's instructions and leave to churn. (Alternatively, pour the mixture into a freezer-proof container, seal with a tight-fitting lid, place in the freezer and remove after 1 hour and whisk; repeat 3 times before leaving to set.)

✳

4. Serve with a piping-hot mug of chai tea or mulled wine.

# Savoury Ice Cream

Traditionally, ice cream was (and remains) a sweet dish, normally served as a dessert, enjoyed at the seaside or eaten on a long, hot summer day. My friends often snuggle up on the sofa with their partners of an evening with a trashy movie and a bowl of ice cream. It's the ultimate comfort food.

Many of the big-brand ice-cream products in our supermarkets are stodgy, rich, sugary flavours crammed with fat and artificial flavourings and colours. One of the reasons I wrote this book was to change opinions about how good, honest and fresh ice cream should taste. Flavours can still be rich and tasty with all of the bad stuff left out.

By writing this book, I went on a journey of discovery myself. Meeting different producers, chefs and ice-cream lovers and foodies opened my mind to different flavour combinations, ingredients and a world of new tastes and textures.

Chefs such as Rob Rees, aka The Cotswold Chef, based in the Roman town of Cirencester, and Chef Dan Ingram of the award-winning Red Lion in Cricklade both suggested trying out savoury ice-cream recipes. I admit that, at first, I was a little reluctant – and I imagine you will be, too. But think outside the box and forget eating ice cream on a waffled cone with a chocolate flake, plastic spoon and toffee sauce; the recipes in this chapter complement salads, meats and seafood. Rather than a sweet topping sauce, consider sprinkling these with black pepper or a splash of balsamic vinegar. It's all about experimenting with different dishes.

*All recipes in this chapter are designed to serve 4–6 people – generously!*

CHEF'S TIP

**Sourcing ingredients**

*Remember where possible to support your local markets and producers
and, if the budget allows, choose organic ingredients.*

# Goats Cheese Ice Cream

My first encounter with goats cheese ice cream was during a visit to a rather fantastic Michelin-starred restaurant in central London. Seeing it on the menu I was totally fascinated and ordered two helpings. The body of flavour, texture and consistency was impressive – so much so that I rushed home to begin experimenting myself. The flavour is surprising and not unpleasant: a good balance between sweet and savoury. Here especially I recommend using local organic goats cheese in order to avoid an overly pungent flavour.

4 large organic egg yolks
120g Fairtrade caster sugar
250ml organic full-fat milk
100ml organic double cream
200g organic goats cheese

1. In a saucepan mix the egg yolks and sugar until a smooth, pale, custard-like paste forms. Slowly begin to heat the custard, using a spatula to stir the mixture almost continuously to avoid burning it as it thickens.

2. In a separate saucepan, heat the milk and cream for approximately 5 minutes before gently pouring it into the egg/custard mixture and mixing well.

3. Crumble the goats cheese into the custard mixture and stir. Gradually increase the heat and continue to stir until all the cheese has melted and combined with the mixture.

4. Set aside to cool, then pour into your ice-cream maker, follow the manufacturer's instructions and leave to churn. (Alternatively, pour the mixture into a freezer-proof container, seal it firmly with a lid and place in the freezer. Whisk after 1 hour to prevent ice crystals from forming; repeat 3 times before leaving it to set.)

# Tomato Ice Cream

A research team in America concluded that the reason we all enjoy different flavours of ice cream is directly linked to the amount of amylase within our saliva and taste buds (amylase is an enzyme that helps break down carbohydrates). I'm sure some readers won't attempt to make or try this recipe, but for you more adventurous types, bear in mind that this recipe is merely a guide: you can adjust the levels of tomato purée, pepper and even add mustard powder to taste. This savoury ice cream is delicious with a seasonal salad and seafood.

15 plum tomatoes, chopped
400ml fresh, organic double cream
tomato purée to taste
5 fresh basil leaves
2–3 tsp olive oil
Freshly ground black pepper, to taste
Lemon juice, to taste
Pinch of sugar

1. Wash, peel and deseed your tomatoes, ensuring you use only fresh, ripe tomatoes full of colour. Roughly chop the tomatoes and put them into a blender along with the cream, 2-3 teaspoons of tomato purée (or more, to taste), the basil leaves and olive oil. Blend until smooth.

※

2. Add the black pepper and lemon juice to taste, and if needed, more tomato purée (I favour organic, of course).

※

3. Blend again to ensure a smooth, consistent mixture. Finish with a pinch of sugar. Pour the mixture through a fine sieve several times.

※

4. Leave the mixture to rest before pouring it into your ice-cream maker. Follow the manufacturer's instructions and leave to churn. (Alternatively, pour the mixture into a freezer-proof container, seal it firmly with a lid and place in the freezer. Whisk after 1 hour to prevent ice crystals from forming; repeat 3 times before leaving it to set.)

# Wasabi Ice Cream

Wasabi is also known as Japanese horseradish and it's fairly obvious why: its strong, peppery flavour is similar to that of chilli, horseradish and mustard, and in fact it's derived from the same family as all three. Wasabi can be bought in its raw root form, as a paste, or more commonly as a condiment/sauce and is readily available from most Asian-Oriental food stores and supermarkets. This recipe is best served like horseradish sauce, with a leafy green salad and red meat, game or chicken.

250ml organic double cream
200ml organic full-fat milk
150g Fairtrade caster sugar
1 large organic egg
50g wasabi paste (adjust to taste)

1. Pour the cream and milk into a dishwasher-friendly saucepan. Tip in half of the sugar and place over a low heat, stirring at regular intervals and not allowing the mixture to boil.

✳

2. Whisk the egg yolk and the remaining sugar in a mixing bowl, beating with an electric whisk for about 2 minutes, or until the mixture has become a smooth, pale paste.

✳

3. Combine both mixtures and return the pan to a low heat. Cook, stirring all the time, for approximately 10 minutes, until the mixture has a thick, custard-like consistency. Add the wasabi paste and continue to stir.

✳

4. Set aside to cool, then pour into your ice-cream maker, follow the manufacturer's instructions and leave to churn. (Alternatively, pour the mixture into a freezer-proof container, seal it firmly with a lid and place in the freezer. Whisk after 1 hour to prevent ice crystals from forming; repeat 3 times before leaving it to set.)

# Jerusalem Artichoke & Nutmeg Ice Cream

Artichoke hearts are common on fine-dining menus due to a revival in their popularity. While they may look somewhat intimidating in their raw form, a skilful peeling reveals a delicious prize that lurks beneath the leafy exterior. This recipe is unique and I recommend serving it with a thin shaving of Parmesan as a sort of 'solid aperitif' – preferably in a shot glass.

500g chopped artichoke
200ml organic full-fat milk
300ml organic double cream
3 large organic eggs
100g Fairtrade caster sugar
Ground nutmeg to taste
Handful of finely chopped mint leaves, to serve

1. Bring a saucepan of salted water to the boil. Add the chopped artichoke and cook for 10 minutes to soften. Drain the water and purée the artichoke in a blender, then put it through a strainer to obtain a fine purée before placing in the refrigerator.

✳

2. Bring the milk and cream to the boil, stirring constantly.

✳

3. Beat the eggs and sugar in a bowl until the mixture is foamy. Gradually add the milk and cream, whisking constantly.

✳

4. Pour the mixture into a saucepan, add the nutmeg and cook over a low heat for 10 minutes, stirring with a spatula in a figure-eight pattern. The mixture must not boil. Cool and refrigerate.

✳

5. When the custard is cold, add the artichoke purée and mix well. Pour into your ice-cream maker, follow the manufacturer's instructions and leave to churn until you get the desired consistency. (Alternatively, pour the mixture into a freezer-proof container, seal it firmly with a lid and place in the freezer. Whisk after 1 hour to prevent ice crystals from forming; repeat 3 times before leaving it to set.)

✳

6. Put the ice cream into a shallow container and add the mint leaves to serve.

# Cracked Black Pepper Ice Cream

Cracked black pepper was first suggested to me as a potential flavour by the fantastic 'Cotswold chef', Rob Rees, who champions quality local artisan producers and farmers. Here, the dry and somewhat spicy flavour of black pepper produces an adaptable ice cream packed full of punch. This flavour can be contrasted with a serving of sweet fruit coulis or served with a Mediterranean main course.

250ml organic double cream
150ml organic full-fat milk
4 medium organic egg yolks
50g Fairtrade caster sugar
1 tbsp cracked black pepper (adjust to taste)

1. Pour the cream and milk into a dishwasher-friendly saucepan and put it over a low heat, stirring at regular intervals to prevent the mixture from boiling or burning.

❋

2. Whisk the egg yolks and sugar together in a mixing bowl, beating with an electric whisk for about 2 minutes, or by hand until the mixture has become a smooth, pale paste. This will form the base of your ice-cream custard mix.

❋

3. Combine the milk/cream and custard mixtures and return the pan to a low heat. Cook, stirring all the time, for approximately 10 minutes, or until the mixture develops a thick, custard-like consistency.

❋

4. Add the black pepper and stir vigorously. Continue to stir for approximately 5 minutes, adding more pepper if needed. Once the custard has thickened, remove it from the heat and set aside to cool.

❋

5. Pour the custard into your ice-cream maker and follow the manufacturer's instructions for churning. (Alternatively, pour it into a freezer-proof container, seal it firmly with a lid and place it in the freezer. Whisk after 1 hour to prevent ice crystals from forming; repeat 3 times before leaving it to set.)

# Honey & Sage Ice Cream

The sweetness of orange-blossom honey and aromatic, well-perfumed taste of fresh sage make for a well-balanced, light and delicate flavour that will sit happily alongside other sweet or savoury dishes. I wholeheartedly encourage you to experiment here; why not try replacing the sage with a different herb, spice or addition? Thyme, perhaps, or parsley – even wild garlic leaves?

300ml organic double cream
2 tsp ground sage
250ml organic full-fat milk
4 large organic egg yolks
100g Fairtrade caster sugar
100g local honey

1. Put the cream, ground sage and milk into a medium dishwasher-friendly saucepan. Gently heat the mixture until it almost boils; you'll see a few bubbles begin to surface. It's important, though, to ensure that the mixture doesn't burn, so remember to stir.

❋

2. Put the egg yolks into a mixing bowl, add the sugar and beat with an electric whisk for about 2 minutes until the mixture becomes a smooth paste. Transfer to a saucepan over a low heat and begin to warm gently.

❋

3. Combine the milk mixture with the custard and return it to the heat. Add the honey into the custard and stir vigorously to combine, then return the saucepan to the heat for approximately 10 minutes.

❋

4. Remove from the heat and set aside to cool.

❋

5. Pour the mixture into your ice-cream maker, follow the manufacturer's instructions and leave to churn. (Alternatively, pour it into a freezer-proof container, seal it firmly with a lid and place in the freezer. Whisk after 1 hour to prevent ice crystals from forming; repeat 3 times before leaving it to set.)

❋

6. Serve with a simple crisp garden salad and citrus dressing.

# Olive Oil Ice Cream

In terms of ice-cream flavours, olive oil is very much in vogue on restaurant menus. This quick-and-easy recipe is packed with flavour and has a gorgeous silky-smooth texture. I recommend serving it as an accompaniment to a salad or gazpacho.

100g Fairtrade caster sugar, plus 1 tsp
250ml organic full-fat milk
100ml water
4 large organic egg yolks
200ml olive oil
1 tsp lemon juice

1. Pour the sugar (apart from the teaspoon), milk and water into a saucepan and simmer for approximately 5 minutes to allow the flavours to infuse. Gradually bring to the boil.

✳

2. Put the egg yolks into a large heatproof bowl with a teaspoon of sugar and beat until combined. Slowly pour in the boiling milk and continue to whisk.

✳

3. Return the mixture to the saucepan and heat until it begins to thicken – enough to coat the back of a spoon. Once thick enough, set aside to cool, then add the olive oil, mixing by hand with a wooden spoon.

✳

4. Set the mixture aside in the refrigerator to chill before pouring into your ice-cream maker. Follow the manufacturer's instructions and leave to churn. (Alternatively, pour it into a freezer-proof container, seal it firmly with a lid and place in the freezer. Whisk after 1 hour to prevent ice crystals from forming; repeat 3 times before leaving it to set.)

✳

5. Serve with a crisp garden salad and citrus dressing or gazpacho.

# Sorbet

Sorbet is a frozen dessert that is similar to ice cream, but without the addition of milk or cream or the need to aerate the mixture. Essentially it sits as a happy medium between ice cream and granita and shares many of the same origins of the former, dating back to the ancient empires of Persia and Rome.

While it's very unlikely that you'll see kids walking around seaside resorts with sorbet in cones or paper pots, you're more likely to have it served between courses at a restaurant as a palate cleanser. That said, sorbets are equally as delicious and refreshing at home on a hot summer day or as the ideal accompaniment to any dinner party.

Different cultures have different names, recipes and styles of sorbet, but my own sorbet recipes are simple and easy to follow – perfect for an impromptu dinner party or any time a last-minute dessert is called for.

And the good news? In most cases sorbet is non- or low-fat: meaning you can enjoy it guilt-free without pounding those pavements afterwards in your dad's 1980s' tracksuit.

All sorbets are relatively cheap to make, require little preparation and are made on the same principle of freezing sugar syrup flavoured with fruit juice, alcohol or purée. Sorbets are also very adaptable. Once you've tried out my method and recipes a few times, you'll find it easy to get creative and experiment with your own sorbets. Just bear in mind that the tarter the fruit, the sweeter the syrup must be to balance its flavour.

*All recipes in this chapter are designed to serve 4–6 people – generously!*

## CHEF'S TIP
### Making sorbet by hand
*Pour the syrup into a freezer-proof container, seal it tightly with a lid and place it in the freezer. Remove after 1 hour to whisk – this stops large ice crystals from forming and should be repeated 3 times before leaving to set. Note: adding a tsp of liquid glucose will make the mixture more scoop-able after freezing.*

# Dark Chocolate Sorbet

Dark chocolate is a great palate-cleanser. Using 200g of Divine Fairtrade 70% chocolate (or any other high-quality alternative), a small amount of sugar and water, you can create this delicious luxury sorbet in less than 30 minutes: perfect for any last-minute dinner party.

50g Fairtrade caster sugar
400ml water
200g quality Fairtrade chocolate, (70%), roughly chopped

1. Pour the sugar and water into a saucepan and place over a medium heat. Stir until all of the sugar has dissolved, then leave to boil for approximately 5 minutes to thicken.

✳

2. Stir in the chocolate until it has melted, then set aside to cool.

✳

3. Pop the mixture into the fridge to chill before pouring it into your ice-cream maker and churning according to the manufacturer's instructions. (Alternatively, pour the mixture into a shallow freezer-proof container, seal it firmly with a lid and freeze it for an 40 minutes. Remove from the freezer and beat with an electric mixer or fork to break up any ice crystals, then return to the freezer. Repeat this procedure at least 3 times before leaving it to set.)

## CHEF'S TIP
### Using Divine Chocolate
*Divine is chocolate that makes everyone feel good. It's 45% owned by cocoa farmers and made for chocolate-lovers and cooks alike. The business was originally set up by the former owners of The Body Shop and has since been handed over to the farmers. I prefer the 70% dark or 85% chocolate bars. Both are full of flavour notes that make them perfect for ice-cream- or sorbet-making. Delicious!*

# Damson & Sloe Vodka Sorbet

Although often similar in appearance, damsons shouldn't be confused with sloes. Both can be dark-purple, but damsons are larger and more plum-like. Sloes grow in the wild on the large shrub *Prunus spinosa* and are ripe to pick from late September onwards. Like damsons, they're tart when eaten raw, but work particularly well when making gin or vodka. While you may have made sloe gin, sloe vodka seems rare by comparison. I first tried sloe vodka at my local pub with fresh fruit, ice and lemonade in a tall glass. It has been my favourite summer drink ever since – and it makes for a great sorbet.

450g ripe damsons
400ml water (plus a few tablespoons)
3 tbsp sloe vodka (or gin)
150g Fairtrade caster sugar

1. Put the damsons, a few tablespoons of water and the sloe vodka (or gin) in a blender and blitz them. Alternatively, reduce them in a saucepan over a medium heat, then push the mixture through a fine sieve.

2. Add the sugar and 400ml water, pour into a saucepan and put over a medium heat to simmer for approximately 10 minutes before setting aside to chill in the fridge. Add lemon juice to taste, if desired; this will bring out the flavours if they taste dull.

3. Pour the mixture into an ice-cream maker and follow the manufacturer's instructions; leave to churn. (Alternatively, pour the sorbet mixture into a shallow freezer-proof container, seal it tightly and freeze for 1 hour. Remove from the freezer and beat with an electric mixer or fork until smooth, then return to the freezer. Repeat this procedure at least 3 times before leaving to set overnight.)

## CHEF'S TIP
### Picking sloes
*The sloe is a fruit of the blackthorn bush, which you'll often find growing in hedgerows near scrub and common land or in woodland. Sloes should be picked around the time of the first frost and make delicious gin, vodka – and sorbet.*

# Elderflower Sorbet

Growing up in Gloucestershire, I have seen local company Bottlegreen expand and develop over the years, blossoming (much like elderflower) into a well-recognised international brand. For me, the company's delicious drinks evoke many happy memories of childhood summers in the countryside. Elderflower is a very delicate flavour, and thus the conservative use of lemon juice here will help it remain, even when the mixture is frozen.

150g Fairtrade caster sugar
500ml water
2 tablespoons fresh lemon juice, strained
50ml elderflower cordial (Bottlegreen or Belvoir)

1. Pour the caster sugar and the water into a small saucepan and place over a medium heat. Heat gently, stirring, until the sugar has completely dissolved. Bring to the boil and boil steadily for 5 minutes (without stirring), or until the solution has attained the consistency of a thin syrup. Leave to cool, then stir in the lemon juice and elderflower cordial; top up to taste.

✳

2. Pour the mixture into an ice-cream maker and follow the manufacturer's instructions. (Alternatively, if you don't have an ice-cream maker, pour the mixture into a shallow freezer-proof container, seal tightly with a lid and freeze for an hour. Remove from the freezer and beat with an electric mixer until smooth, then return to the freezer. Repeat this procedure at least 3 times to produce a smooth, fine-textured sorbet, then leave it to freeze until very firm.)

✳

3. Serve in a cocktail glass with a few slices of fresh fruit.

# Elderflower & Champagne Sorbet

The Bottlegreen drinks company is based just outside the town of Nailsworth, in Gloucestershire. During the summer the firm encouraged locals (including us children) to pick elderflower from back gardens, local fields and hedgerows in exchange for money. My mother sent my brother and me out to fill a refuse sack, and we'd get to spend the few pounds we made on whatever we liked – usually a trip to the sweet shop. Here sweet, fragrant elderflower lends itself well to the Champagne's flavour notes to make a delicious sorbet worth celebrating!

3 tbsp lemon juice
250ml water
150g Fairtrade caster sugar
4 tbsp elderflower cordial (I use Bottlegreen or Belvoir)
200ml Champagne

1. Pour the lemon juice, water, sugar and elderflower cordial into a small saucepan. Stir well, then heat gently until the sugar dissolves. Bring the pan to the boil, then remove it from the heat and allow to cool to room temperature. As the mixture cools, it will thicken to a sugar syrup.

❋

2. Add the Champagne, stir, then transfer to an ice-cream maker and churn following the manufacturer's instructions. (Alternatively, pour the syrup into a freezer-proof container, seal it tightly wit a lid and place in the freezer. Remove after 1 hour to whisk – this stops large ice crystals from forming and should be repeated 3 times before leaving to set. Note: adding a tsp of liquid glucose will make the mixture more scoop-able after freezing.) Once churning is complete transfer to the freezer for a couple of hours to allow the sorbet to harden.

❋

3. Serve in a cocktail or shot glass garnished with a sliced strawberry.

# English Tea Sorbet

As the philosopher Bernard-Paul Heroux once said, 'There is no trouble so great or grave that cannot be much diminished by a nice cup of tea.' A nice sentiment indeed! In English Tea Sorbet I've used prune juice, Earl Grey tea and lemon to make a refreshing, aromatic combination and palate-cleanser when served alongside generous helpings of fresh summer fruit.

200g Fairtrade caster sugar
300ml water
4 Earl Grey tea bags
500g prune juice
Half a fresh organic lemon

1. Pour the caster sugar and water into a small saucepan and place over a medium-low heat.

✳

2. Drop the tea bags into the water and heat slowly, stirring, until the sugar has completely dissolved. Bring to the boil and boil steadily for 5 minutes (without stirring), or until the solution has attained the consistency of a thin syrup. Leave to cool to allow the aromatic flavour of the tea to infuse.

✳

3. After 30 minutes or so, remove the tea bags from the syrup, squeezing out all of the remaining liquid from them before adding the prune juice and lemon juice to taste.

✳

4. Pour the mixture into an ice-cream maker and follow the manufacturer's instructions. (Alternatively, pour the mixture into a shallow freezer-proof container, seal it tightly with a lid and freeze for 1 hour. Remove from the freezer and beat with an electric mixer until smooth, then return to the freezer. Repeat this procedure at least 3 times to produce a smooth, fine-textured sorbet, then leave to freeze until very firm.)

# Gin & Tonic Sorbet

The long drink known as gin and tonic was originally developed as a medicine to help fight malaria. During the British colonial period in the Far East, soldiers became susceptible to malaria and it was eventually discovered that quinine, an ingredient in tonic water, was useful for treating the disease. History aside, this summer drink makes for a refreshing and interesting sorbet. Serve it with a slice of lemon or lime.

200g Fairtrade caster sugar
300ml water
250ml tonic water
125ml lemonade
50ml gin (or to taste)
2 tbsp lemon juice

1. Put the sugar and water into a saucepan, bring to the boil and simmer for 1 minute. The mixture will thicken to a syrup. Set aside to cool.

❊

2. Mix in the tonic water and lemonade, then put the syrup in the fridge to chill.

❊

3. Add the gin and lemon juice to taste. Be conservative here with the gin; when frozen, its flavour intensifies, and if the alcohol content is too high, the mixture won't freeze. Mix well.

❊

4. Pour into your ice-cream maker and follow the manufacturer's instructions. Alternatively, simply pour the sorbet mixture into a freezer-friendly container, seal with a tight-fitting lid and put it in the freezer. Remove the sorbet from the freezer every hour or so, whisk it until the ice crystals are broken down and the consistency is smooth, then put back into freezer.
Repeat 3 times before leaving to set solid.)

# Lime & Basil Sorbet

Sorbets should cleanse the palate, be refreshing and give a clean, crisp flavour. Basil & Lime Sorbet is no exception: this well-balanced flavour works perfectly between courses and would be right at home at any cocktail party or evening do. Adjust the flavour to taste; the addition of lemon juice will help bring out the flavours and give the lime more of a kick.

150g Fairtrade caster sugar
200ml water
Juice of 6 limes
2–3 teaspoons of lemon juice
Large bunch of basil

1. Put the caster sugar and the water in a small saucepan and place over a medium-low heat. Heat the pan gently, stirring, until the sugar has completely dissolved. Bring to the boil and boil steadily for 5 minutes (without stirring), or until the solution has attained the consistency of a thin syrup. Set aside to cool.

✳

2. As the sugar syrup begins to cool, stir in the lime juice and lemon juice.

✳

3. Crush the basil to a pulp using a pestle and mortar, or finely chop it. Mix it in with lime syrup and return to the heat for 5 minutes to allow the flavours to infuse. Set aside to cool.

✳

4. Pour the mixture into an ice-cream maker and follow the manufacturer's instructions. (Alternatively, pour it into a shallow, freezer-proof container, seal with a tight-fitting lid and freeze for 1 hour. Remove from the freezer and beat with an electric mixer until smooth, then return to the freezer. Repeat this procedure 3 times to produce a smooth, fine-textured sorbet, then leave to freeze until very firm.)

✳

5. Serve in scoops and garnish with a basil leaf.

# Lemon Vodka Sorbet

Whenever I host a dinner party I often serve lemon sorbet between courses, or straight after mains in anticipation of a big dessert. It's typically Sicilian and a fantastic way to cleanse the palate. In fact, the intense taste – in between sweet and acid – makes it a perfect 'cleanser'. This recipe is extremely easy and takes only about half an hour to make. I prefer the exquisite Chase Vodka, but you can use the vodka of your choice.

200g Fairtrade caster sugar
300ml water
250ml strained lemon juice (about 5 large lemons)
A dash of freshly squeezed lime juice
3 tbsp lemon vodka

1. Put the caster sugar and water in a small saucepan and place over a medium-low heat. Heat the pan gently, stirring, until the sugar has completely dissolved. Bring to the boil and boil steadily for 5 minutes (without stirring), or until the solution has attained the consistency of a thin syrup. Set aside to cool, then stir in the lemon juice, lime juice and vodka.

❋

2. Pour the mixture into an ice-cream maker and follow the manufacturer's instructions. Alternatively, pour it into a shallow freezer-proof container, seal with a tight-fitting lid and freeze for an hour. Remove from the freezer and beat with a fork to break up ice crystals, then return it to the freezer. Repeat this procedure at least 3 times to produce a smooth, fine-textured sorbet, then leave to freeze until very firm.)

❋

3. Serve scoops in a shot glass and decorate with strips of lemon peel.

## CHEF'S TIP
### Choosing the perfect vodka
*I always use Chase Vodka. Based in Herefordshire, William Chase, the chap who started the delicious Tyrell's crisp brand, makes vodka using the finest home-grown potatoes. It's smooth – and it's British, so fits in with my locally sourcing ethos.*

# Orange Sorbet

This simple but very refreshing and easy-to-make orange sorbet can also be made with clementines or peaches, or both. Preparation time is approximately 15 minutes, and once ready, it should be served in a glass bowl or dish and topped with orange peel or candied clementine.

200g Fairtrade caster sugar
400ml water
400ml freshly squeezed orange juice
Dash of lemon juice

1. Pour the caster sugar and the water into a small saucepan and place over a medium-low heat. Heat the pan gently, stirring, until the sugar has completely dissolved. Bring to the boil and boil steadily for 5 minutes (without stirring), or until the solution has attained the consistency of a thin syrup. Leave to cool.

✳

2. Stir in the orange juice, and just a dash of lemon juice.

✳

3. Pour the mixture into an ice-cream maker and follow the manufacturer's instructions. (Alternatively, pour into a freezer-safe container, seal with a tight-fitting lid and put in the freezer. Remove from the freezer after 1 hour to whisk – this stops large ice crystals from forming and should be repeated 3 times before leaving to set.)

✳

4. Once the churning cycle is complete, decant into a freezer-safe container and freeze for up to 4 hours to ensure the sorbet is adequately frozen.

# Raspberry Sorbet

Aside from being super-tasty and growing all over the countryside, raspberries are super fruits with loads of nutritional benefits. For starters they're packed with antioxidants (50 per cent more than strawberries) and are fibre-rich. Kids of all ages totally love the deep-purple hue (not to mention the sweet, tart, tongue-tingling feeling), so find fresh raspberries in season at farmers' markets or grow your own. Then, bring out the ice-cream maker for some fun family sorbet-crafting!

100g Fairtrade caster sugar
200ml water
500g fresh raspberries
Juice of 1 fresh lemon

1. Put the caster sugar and the water in a small saucepan and place over a medium-low heat. Heat the pan gently, stirring, until the sugar has completely dissolved. Bring to the boil and boil steadily for 5 minutes (without stirring), or until the solution has attained the consistency of a thin syrup.

※

2. Put the raspberries in another pan. Squeeze some lemon juice over them (to taste) and simmer over a low heat for 1–2 minutes until soft, then pour the softened raspberries into a blender and purée until smooth.

※

3. Push the purée through a fine sieve to remove all the seeds – which would otherwise give the sorbet a sharp, bitter taste.

※

4. Pour the mixture into an ice-cream maker, follow the manufacturer's instructions and leave to churn. (Alternatively, pour into a freezer-safe container, seal with a tight-fitting lid and put in the freezer. Remove from the freezer after 1 hour to whisk – this stops large ice crystals from forming and should be repeated 3 times before leaving to set.)

※

5. Once the cycle is complete decant into a freezer-safe container and freeze for up to 4 hours to ensure the sorbet is adequately frozen.

# Strawberry & Champagne Sorbet

My first experience of Strawberry & Champagne Sorbet was at the Henley Regatta in Henley-on-Thames, Oxfordshire. The event, in which international crews row against each other, dates back to the 1800s. One year I was lucky enough to come across this fantastic sorbet at one of the food exhibits, made using vintage Bollinger Champagne. You can use any decent fizz you like for this, but be sure to serve it with fresh fruit to accompany a light meal.

250g Fairtrade caster sugar
200ml water
200g strawberries
2 tsp lemon juice
250ml quality Champagne

1. Put the caster sugar and the water in a small saucepan and place over a medium-low heat. Heat the pan gently, stirring, until the sugar has completely dissolved. Bring to the boil and boil steadily for 5 minutes (without stirring), or until the solution has attained the consistency of a thin syrup. Remove from the heat and set aside to cool.

❋

2. Put the fresh strawberries in a blender. Add the lemon juice and a splash of water and blend until you have a smooth purée.

❋

3. Add the strawberry purée and the Champagne to the sugar syrup, stir to mix, then return to a medium-low heat for a further 5 minutes to allow the flavours to infuse.

❋

4. Pour the mixture into an ice-cream maker and follow the manufacturer's instructions. (Alternatively, pour the mixture into a shallow freezer-proof container and freeze for 1 hour. Remove from the freezer and beat with an electric mixer until smooth, then return to the freezer. Repeat this procedure 3 times to produce a smooth, fine-textured sorbet, then leave to freeze until very firm.)

❋

5. Serve in Champagne flutes and garnish with slices of fresh strawberry.

# Summer Pimm's Sorbet

Pimm's was first made in 1823 by James Pimm, a farmer's son from just outside Kent. The drink was designed as a tonic: gin-based with quinine (similar to a G&T) but with a secret mixture of herbs and fruit included that Pimm thought would aid digestion. He served it in a small tankard known as a 'No. 1 Cup' – a name that has stuck to this day. Nowadays it's usually enjoyed in a tall glass with ice, lashings of lemonade and fresh fruit –and don't forget the cucumber! This sorbet incorporates Pimm's in the mix, and it's equally as refreshing on a hot summer's day.

125g Fairtrade caster sugar
125ml lemonade
10 tbsp Pimm's No.1 Cup
100ml water
2 tbsp lemon juice
300g fresh strawberries
50g fresh cucumber

1. Pour the caster sugar, lemonade, Pimm's and water into a small saucepan and place it over a medium-low heat. Heat the pan gently, stirring, until all of the sugar has completely dissolved. Bring to the boil and boil steadily for 5 minutes (without stirring), or until the solution has attained the consistency of a thin syrup. Remove from the heat and set aside to cool, then stir in the lemon juice.

✳

2. Put the strawberries and cucumber in a blender and blend until a you have a smoothie-like substance. Leave it to settle for 5 minutes.

✳

3. Add the fruit mixture to the syrup and place over a medium heat for 5–10 minutes, stirring to combine the ingredients. Set aside to cool.

✳

4. Pour into an ice-cream maker and follow the manufacturer's instructions. (Alternatively, pour it into a shallow freezer-proof container, seal with a tight-fitting lid and freeze for 1 hour. Remove from the freezer and beat with an electric mixer until smooth, then return it to the freezer. Repeat this procedure 3 times to produce a smooth, fine-textured sorbet, then leave to freeze until very firm.)

✳

5. Serve with fruit in a glass bowl, garnished with a few mint leaves.

# Winter Pimm's Sorbet

This is a simple, seasonal take on my classic summer Pimm's sorbet recipe on page 152 – perfect for cold, dark nights with a fruit crumble and a piping-hot glass of mulled wine.

125g Fairtrade caster sugar
10 tbsp Pimm's Winter Cup
100ml water
1 tsp of cinnamon
50g blended fresh apple
250g blended winter fruit (figs, plums, blackberries, raspberries, quinces, pears, etc)

1. Pour the caster sugar, Pimm's and water into a small saucepan and place over a medium-low heat. Heat the pan gently, stirring, until all of the sugar has completely dissolved. Bring to the boil and boil steadily for 5 minutes (without stirring), or until the solution has attained the consistency of a thin syrup. Set aside to cool.

❋

2. In a blender, purée the apples, cinnamon and winter fruit until you have a smoothie-like substance. Leave to settle for 5 minutes, then check the flavour. If it's dull, add a few teaspoons of lemon juice to taste.

❋

3. Combine the fruit mixture with the syrup and put over a medium heat for 5-10 minutes, ensuring all of the mixture is well combined before pouring into an ice-cream maker.

❋

4. Follow the manufacturer's instructions and leave to churn. (Alternatively, pour the mixture into a shallow freezer-proof container, seal with a tight-fitting lid and freeze for 1 hour. Remove from the freezer and beat with an electric mixer until smooth, then return to the freezer. Repeat this procedure 3 times to produce a smooth, fine-textured sorbet, then leave to freeze until very firm.)

❋

5. Serve in a shot glass with winter fruit.

# Semifreddo

Semifreddo is a simple, easy-to-make frozen dessert that originated in Italy, where it remains popular. In Italian, *semifreddo* translates as 'semi-frozen' or 'half-frozen'. As a dessert it falls halfway between mousse and ice cream. While it's much lighter than ice cream and melts in the mouth, semifreddo production is much like French-style of ice-cream making. Unlike ice cream, semifreddo doesn't need added air, which means it doesn't need churning in an ice-cream maker (or whisking by hand).

Instead, semifreddo is made by gently whipping cream into a thicker base that contains all of a recipe's flavourings (it can be flavoured with just about anything, including fruit, alcohol, chocolate and nuts). This base could consist of a thick custard (similar to a regular ice-cream base used throughout the book) that has been lightened with egg whites, or a much airier meringue. Once mixed, it's simply poured into a loaf tin and frozen for a few hours until it solidifies.

Semifreddo is often sliced like a cake to serve, rather than being scooped like ice cream. I prefer slicing it and adding a generous helping of fresh fruit and cream. Thanks to its light consistency, semifreddo is often served this way, because its texture makes cutting through it with a knife very simple.

The big advantage of semifreddo is that it requires no special equipment to make; it's just as simple and straightforward as the sorbets found on pages 133–53. They come together quickly and can be served within a few hours.

In this chapter I present a variety of simple, quick and easy-to-make semifreddo recipes ranging from Divine Chocolate to Neapolitan, both of which are particular favourites of mine.

*All recipes in this chapter are designed to serve 4–6 people – generously!*

# Divine Chocolate Semifreddo

If you've already made any of the chocolate ice cream or sorbet recipes in this book, then it's likely that you'll have some leftover ingredients that will also work here. Also, if you're looking for a delicious and quick dessert recipe, then this is the one for you. Serve it sliced with Rich Chocolate Sauce (164) or Hot Toffee Fudge Sauce (see page 167) and a generous helping of fresh fruit.

200ml organic full-fat milk
100g Fairtrade caster sugar
100g Divine chocolate (70% or higher), roughly chopped
500ml organic double cream
2 large organic egg yolks

1. Line the base of a loaf tin with baking parchment.

✳

2. Heat the milk and half of the sugar in a saucepan over a medium heat, stirring until the sugar has completely dissolved.

✳

3. Add the chocolate and continue to heat until it has melted.

✳

4. Using an electric whisk, whip the double cream, egg yolks and the remaining caster sugar together. Continue to whisk until the mixture is light, fluffy and forms soft peaks.

✳

5. Gently fold the chocolate mixture into the whipped cream, taking care not to beat the air out of the cream. Decant the mixture into the loaf tin and freeze it for at least 5 hours or overnight. Serve sliced, drizzled with Rich Chocolate Sauce (see page 164).

# Limoncello & Strawberry Semifreddo

Limoncello is a liqueur that was originally made in the southern regions of Italy, most notably Naples, the Amalfi coast and Sicily, using the peel of Sorrento lemons . Its fresh, lemony taste blends perfectly with the lashings of cream and juicy strawberries that make up this semifreddo. Serve it sliced, drizzled with orange-blossom honey and summer fruits.

100g fresh organic strawberries
Dash of lemon juice
4 tbsp water
500ml organic double cream
100g Fairtrade caster sugar
4 tbsp limoncello

1. Line the base of a loaf tin with baking parchment.

❄

2. Purée the strawberries in a blender, then add the lemon juice and water and blend until smooth. Set aside to allow the flavours to infuse.

❄

3. Using a balloon or electric whisk, whisk the cream, caster sugar and limoncello until the mixture forms soft peaks.

❄

4. Pour the strawberry mixture into the cream and give it a few gentle stirs – just enough to swirl it through the creamy mix but without removing any of the air from the cream.

❄

5. Pour the mixture into the loaf tin and smooth the top, then freeze for at least 4 hours. Serve with strawberry coulis.

## CHEF'S TIP
### Strawberry coulis
*Put 200g of fresh strawberries, 2 tbsp of sugar and 4 tbsp of water in a saucepan over a low heat and reduce until soft. Mash through a fine sieve, return to the heat for just a couple of minutes and serve over a thick slice of semifreddo.*

# Mocha Semifreddo

Walk into almost any coffee shop and order a mocha and you'll be served a tall coffee glass of one-third espresso, two-thirds frothy steamed milk with a sprinkling of chocolate and a biscotti to complement – delicious! This semifreddo is equally as delicious, as it retains the same rich body of flavour from the coffee and the creaminess of the milk. Once ready, slice it and serve with biscotti.

100ml organic full-fat milk
150g Fairtrade caster sugar
3 medium organic eggs, separated
400ml organic double cream
2 tbsp quality cocoa powder
25ml freshly brewed espresso
Amaretti biscuits, to serve

1. Line the base of a loaf tin with baking parchment.

※

2. Heat the milk and half the sugar in a saucepan over a medium heat, stirring until the sugar has completely dissolved.

※

3. Using a hand whisk, whip the egg yolks with remaining sugar until thick and light. In another bowl, whip the double cream until stiff. Add the cold espresso and cocoa powder to the cream, then combine both mixtures.

※

4. In a clean bowl whip the egg whites to soft peaks, then gently fold them into the egg-yolk mixture.

※

5. Pour the mixture into the prepared loaf pan, cover and freeze for at least 4 hours. Serve sliced with a crushed amaretti biscuit on top.

# Neapolitan Semifreddo

Preparation is the key here, because this semifreddo will take some time to make.

150g Fairtrade caster sugar
2 large organic egg whites
500ml organic double cream
2 tsp vanilla essence or extract
200g fresh local strawberries
150g fresh local raspberries
50g icing sugar
100g Divine chocolate (70% or higher)

1. Line the base of a loaf tin with baking parchment.

*

2. Pour the caster sugar into a saucepan with a few tablespoons of water, then heat very gently until it has completely dissolved.

*

3. Whisk the egg whites to stiff peaks in a heatproof bowl. When the hot sugar syrup is ready, carefully pour it into the egg whites, a little at a time, whisking until it has all been mixed in and forms soft, fluffy peaks. Set aside to cool.

*

4. Gently whip the cream and vanilla in another bowl. Fold the cream into the egg whites to make the semifreddo base. Divide the mixture into 3 equal parts in 3 different bowls.

*

5. Purée the berries with the icing sugar until smooth. Pass through a sieve over the first third of semifreddo, then fold in until evenly pink. Spoon into the lined tin, level it, then cover the surface with a rectangle of baking parchment. Freeze for 40 minutes.

*

6. Remove the paper and spoon over a layer of plain vanilla mix. Again, level, cover and freeze as before.

*

7. Meanwhile, melt the chocolate over a pan of simmering water, then leave it until it cools but is still runny.

*

8. Fold the chocolate into the remaining semifreddo base. Layer it on top of the vanilla layer, smooth over as before and freeze for at least 4 hours – or overnight before serving. Serve sliced with fresh fruit.

# Orange-blossom Honey Semifreddo

Orange-blossom honey is delicious at any time – but I've included it in this recipe in case you have leftover honey from making the honey-based ice cream flavours in previous chapters (see pages 86, 114, 130). This recipe is simple and straightforward to make, and being semifreddo, it doesn't require you to make a time-consuming custard base. Once made, leave it to freeze overnight, and finish it with a fresh honey and hazelnut topping.

1 egg
4 egg yolks
100g orange-blossom honey (or other quality local honey )
300ml organic double cream
Handful of crushed hazelnuts

1. Line a loaf tin with baking parchment.

※

2. Beat the egg and egg yolks with the honey in a heatproof bowl, then place it over a saucepan of gently simmering water. Warm until the mixture is pale, smooth and thick.

※

3. Whip the double cream until thick, light and fluffy, then gently fold in the egg-and-honey mixture.

※

4. Pour into the loaf tin, and place into the freezer for at least 4 hours, or overnight.

※

5. When ready to serve, turn the semifreddo out on to a plate and drizzle with more honey, then sprinkle with the crushed hazelnuts. Serve in thick slices.

# Toppings

It always disappoints me a bit when, after labouring over a hot stove to create a beautiful, well-balanced and delicate ice cream, people seem so happy to drown it in a sauce or syrup. For this reason, I've put together a number of easy-to-make toppings that won't ruin your ice cream but will simply enhance its flavour. And all of them aim to make use of your leftover ingredients.

The following recipes are all best served hot, and can be made in a medium saucepan over a low heat. Remember to stir almost continuously to avoid burning.

# Butterscotch Sauce

Constant attention is needed here to avoid burning the sugar or cream.
Serve hot over any sweet ice cream.

50g Fairtrade caster sugar
50g Fairtrade brown caster sugar
150g golden syrup
150g organic double cream
1 tsp vanilla extract

In a saucepan, combine all of the ingredients and heat gently before eventually bringing close to the boil. Avoid boiling the mixture. If needed, add a small amount of water to thin it to the desired consistency.

# Rich Chocolate Sauce

This unadulterated rich sauce perfectly complements simple ice-cream flavours such as clotted cream, vanilla, chocolate, mint and even strawberry.

50g butter, softened
150g Fairtrade caster sugar
1 tsp vanilla extract
100g high-quality chocolate (at least 70% cocoa solids)

1. Put a few tablespoons of water, the butter, sugar and vanilla extract in a small saucepan and heat.

＊

2. Melt the chocolate in a bain-marie (or a heatproof bowl placed over a saucepan of simmering water) then add it to the butter mixture.

＊

3. Return the mixture to the heat for approximately 5-10 minutes to melt, but avoid burning it. Serve hot.

# Cider Topping Sauce

Experiment with different ciders and perries to match this with different ice creams and sorbets. Here I've used a sweet cider to create a flavoursome sauce.

50g Fairtrade caster sugar
550ml local sweet cider (or perry)
2 tbsp fresh lemon juice
1 tsp ground cinnamon

Combine all of the ingredients in a saucepan and heat for 5 minutes to ensure they're adequately combined.

# Raspberry Sauce

Too much raspberry can often yield an intensely bitter taste that's wholly unpleasant; thus I advise being conservative with the use of raspberry sauce and avoid pairing it with other bitter flavours. Instead, contrast the bitterness by pouring it over a much sweeter strawberry ice cream or fairly plain vanilla.

250g fresh raspberries
50g Fairtrade caster sugar
50ml water
1 tsp fresh lemon juice

Put all the ingredients in a blender and blitz until smooth, then pour into a saucepan and place over a low heat for 5 minutes to ensure all of the ingredients have combined. Serve hot or cold.

# Sharp Lemon Sauce

This sauce will complement a wide range of different flavours, including sharp, citrus-based sorbets or lemon ice cream, but it works particularly well with my Honey & Ginger Ice Cream on page 114.

400ml water
150g Fairtrade caster sugar
Juice of 4 large organic lemons
A dash of orange juice, to taste

1. Pour the water and sugar into a saucepan and heat gently;
the mixture should thicken into a sugar syrup.

❋

2. Add the lemon juice and a dash of orange juice to taste, stir to mix
thoroughly and serve hot.

# Hot Toffee Fudge Sauce

A generous helping of piping-hot toffee sauce is irresistible – and it's probably the real reason why I wrote this syrup/topping sauce section. This sauce is a true classic: devilishly rich, smooth and gloopy, and best of all it's so simple to make! Don't be shy; enjoy this Winstone classic over almost all the sweet ice-cream recipes in this book.

150ml organic double cream
50g Fairtrade brown caster sugar
Knob of butter, softened
1 tsp vanilla extract
1 tbsp high-quality cocoa powder
25–50g crushed toffee

1. Put the cream, brown caster sugar and butter in a saucepan and place over a low heat, stirring to avoid letting the mixture burn or separate.

✳

2. Add the vanilla extract and cocoa powder and taste. If the mixture doesn't begin to thicken, or the flavour is too subtle, don't be shy: add another teaspoon of brown sugar and adjust accordingly.

✳

3. Add the crushed toffee, stirring it into the mixture. Once melted and thoroughly combined, serve piping hot over ice cream.

# Orange Sauce

This sauce will complement a wide range of different flavours, including sharp, citrus-based sorbets or lemon ice cream, but it also works particularly well with any of my chocolate-based ice-cream recipes, evoking a flavour not too dissimilar to that of Terry's Chocolate Orange!

400ml water
175g Fairtrade caster sugar
Juice of 4 large organic oranges
A dash of lemon juice, to taste

1. Pour the water and sugar into a saucepan and heat gently. The mixture should thicken and become a sugar syrup.

❋

2. Add the fresh orange juice and a dash of lemon juice to taste, stir to mix thoroughly and serve.

# Finishing Touches

## Serving suggestions

Presentation, presentation, presentation: without sounding like a Tony Blair speech from the 1990s, I am, of course, talking about how to present your ice cream, sorbet, semifreddo and granita. After making your sweet treats with such passion, slaving over a hot stove, waiting in anticipation as the ice-cream maker churns away and staring at your pile of washing up in horror, it would be a crime not to finish off your masterpiece to the best of your ability. Whether it's a blondie, brownie, penny lick, ice-cream cone, waffled wafer, meringue nest, oatmeal bed or just a bowl, this is my short guide to good presentation.

### Meringue nests

When making the majority of the ice-cream recipes in the book, you'll find yourself with leftover egg whites. Consider using them up by creating simple meringue nests in which to present your ice cream – or even for use in an Eton mess.

### Cones

While it's entirely possible to make ice-cream cones and wafers at home, the equipment is generally expensive, and the process is complex and time-consuming. For this reason, I recommend buying pre-baked ice-cream cones – the smaller and crisper, the better!

### Other ideas

When selecting the most appropriate means to serve your ice cream at home, bear in mind the size, shape and colour of the dish in comparison to your chosen flavour. Perhaps consider presenting your ice cream – whether it's a fruit flavour such as strawberry, a simple flavour such as vanilla or clotted cream, or a chocolate-based flavour – alongside or on top of rich, moist brownies, together with a generous scoop of clotted cream.

Sorbets can be served both after and during dinner, in either a shot glass or fine cocktail glass, garnished with a slice of fruit or a mint leaf.

# Storing ice cream & sorbet

Commercial ice cream bought from the supermarket will, in many cases, have a shelf life of between six months to a year. This is thanks largely to the chemical stabilisers and sugar added to it that ensure longevity and stability within the ice-cream mix.

When making ice cream in a home environment, you replace commercial stabilisers with huge amounts of sugar with eggs. The white and yolk of an egg are pure genius; we can thank Mother Nature for engineering eggs, because not only does the addition of egg help to stabilise ice cream, giving it a perfect texture, it also helps to emulsify it, which helps extend its freezer life.

If made correctly and stored in a suitable container with a lid, your ice cream should happily last up to three months in the freezer. However, this can't be guaranteed with the Guinness and Baileys recipes on pages 90 and 78; they seem to lose flavour and texture after just a few weeks.

As with all recipes I would advise making a fresh batch if you're expecting friends or family around for dinner. Failure to store your ice cream adequately – namely without an airtight lid – will result in the formation of large ice crystals, and these are unpleasant in both taste and texture.

# Smoothies, Milkshakes & Thickies

This final chapter explores a number of quick, simple smoothie, milkshake and 'thickies' recipes. These complement the ice-cream recipes, and will help you to use up any 'leftovers', because in the process of making my ice creams you'll often find yourself with a number of surplus ingredients: egg whites, fruit, sugar or dairy produce. Also, because seasonality is so important, it's worth noting that almost all fruit, including blackberries, raspberries, strawberries, sloes and damsons, can be put into a freezer-safe container and frozen. This means that if I fancy making Blackberries & Cream Ice Cream (see page 42) or a batch of Strawberry (see page 36) in January or February, then I can, without having to pop to my local supermarket and buy imported fruits that often lack flavour and fresh taste, or else have been sprayed or waxed.

The next few easy-to-follow recipes are my take on smoothies and thickies and will help you make use of your fruit, milk, cream and ice cream. Much like the toppings found on pages 163–69, they need very little preparation, equipment or cooking; however, a blender/juicer will be needed in order to achieve consistency. Meanwhile, get some ice ready and if necessary, sweeten anything to taste with a small amount of locally sourced honey.

*All recipes in this chapter are designed to serve 3–4 people – generously!*

# Smoothies

Smoothies are blended, chilled and most commonly sweetened drinks made using fresh or frozen fruit (and sometimes vegetables), often with the addition of crushed ice or ice cream to provide the desired texture as well as add flavour and body. In many cases honey, chocolate and other ingredients can be added to smoothies to help create a wealth of different flavours (much like ice cream).

If you've somehow missed the smoothie revolution that has taken coffee shops, cafés and supermarket shelves by storm, then firstly you need to know that smoothies are quite simply a quick and easy way to use up surplus fruit, yoghurt, milk and/or ice cream. Plus, they're just darn good fun to make and experiment with in the kitchen.

Just as with ice cream, smoothies are great to make, whether by yourself, with friends or even with the kids – and for the health-conscious, they are also a simple, delicious and (best of all) quick way to get the recommend five-a-day portions of fruit (or even veg).

My interest in smoothies stemmed from ice cream, and was helped in no small measure by Innocent smoothies. Innocent makes a wide range of delicious drinks from fine ingredients. I am especially interested in the potential health benefits of drinking smoothies and thickies, particularly using fruits rich in antioxidants and vitamins. In my own recipes I've replaced the usual cream and ice with ice cream (of course!), not only in the hope that it will encourage you to make some of the downright brilliant ice-cream recipes in this book, but also to help you make use of what you may already have in your freezer.

As a bonus, I've found smoothies to be the easiest, most effective way to encourage kids to learn about, and eat, a whole farmload of different fruit and vegetables. Sneaky, I know, but it really does work!

# Apple & Elderflower Smoothie

Apple and elderflower complement each other very well to make a lovely smoothie, reminiscent of crisp, clean spring flavours – but happily enjoyed all year round! Consider using any leftover crab apples you might have from my Crab Apple & Elderflower Ice Cream (page 67), or maybe even use some cider apples if you're feeling adventurous.
This recipe will makes one very generous portion.

1 tsp fresh lemon juice
2 tbsp elderflower cordial
50ml water
6 apples, washed and sliced
100ml organic Greek yoghurt
A handful of ice

1. Put all of the ingredients (including ice) into a blender and blend for up to 5 minutes, or until well combined.

✳

2. Serve over ice in a tall glass and garnish with a sprig of mint.

# Apple, Pear, Honey & Ginger Smoothie

As a combination, apples, pears, honey and ginger work surprisingly well in a smoothie, even if the flavour is a little delicate. It's easy to overpower the smoothie with ginger, though, so be generous with the lemon juice and Greek yoghurt. Try adjusting the recipe and use cinnamon instead of ginger; it's equally as tasty. This recipe makes two good-sized portions.

1 tsp fresh lemon juice
3 organic pears, washed and sliced
3 tbsp orange-blossom honey
100ml organic apple juice
½ tsp ground ginger
A few handfuls of ice

1. Put all of the ingredients (including ice) into a blender and blend for up to 5 minutes, or until well combined.

※

2. Serve over ice in a tall glass. Totally fresh and delicious!

# Blackberry, Raspberry & Blueberry Smoothie

This recipe is truly divine. In fact, it's sublime. Given all the leftover fresh blackberries and raspberries you may have already picked for use in the ice-cream recipes, this smoothie should be very low-cost. I'm sure you don't need me to tell you just how good these three berries are for your health and well being – so I won't. Instead, I'll just remind you that this is the easy way to your five-a-day, so enjoy! This recipe makes at least four generous servings.

1 tsp fresh lemon juice
200g fresh local blackberries
100g fresh raspberries
100g fresh blueberries
2 organic apples, washed and sliced
1 Fairtrade banana
A few handfuls of ice

1. Wash all your fruit, put everything into your blender and go hell-for-leather for at least 5 minutes.

❄

2. Serve over ice in a tall glass.

# Strawberry & Banana Smoothie

This smoothie is a classic in our family. It was sold in our ice-cream parlour for years, until it became so popular that we just couldn't source enough Greek yoghurt! It's simple, tasty and covers three of your recommended five-a-day portions of fruit. Feel free to replace the Greek yoghurt with low-fat or even fat-free yoghurt (for the health-conscious of you out there). Makes two generous portions.

2 organic apples
12 fresh strawberries
1 Fairtrade banana, sliced
Half an orange
50ml organic Greek yoghurt
Handful of ice

1. Wash all your fruit, slice it, take out any nasty pips and chuck everything else into your blender. Blend on full speed for at least 5 minutes.

※

2. Serve over ice in a tall glass.

# Summer Smoothie

For a delicious taste of summer, this recipe will provide you with
three very generous portions.

150g fresh local strawberries, washed and hulled
50g fresh local blackberries
50g blueberries
50g raspberries
3 organic apples
1 tsp fresh lemon juice
100ml organic Greek yoghurt
A handful of ice

Wash all your fruit, remove any nasty bits, then whizz everything up in your blender for up to 5 minutes and feel the power! Once smooth and fully combined, adjust to taste, adding more yoghurt or strawberries if the smoothie is too sour. And bingo! There you have it: one nutritious, delicious and downright summery smoothie!